The New
VEGETARIAN
Cookbook

The New VEGETARIAN Cookbook

Roz Denny

HERMES HOUSE

This imprint published by Hermes House in 2002

Hermes House is an imprint of Anness Publishing Limited
Hermes House 88–89 Blackfriars Road, London SE1 8HA

Published in the USA by Hermes House, Anness Publishing Inc
27 West 20th Street, New York, NY 10011

Publisher: Joanna Lorenz
Project Editor: Jack Straw
Designer: Adrian Morris
Photographer: Michael Michaels
Home Economist: Wendy Lee
Production Controller: Joanna King

Printed and bound in Singapore

NOTE:
Some vegetarians may prefer not to use Worcestershire sauce in cooking,
in which case mushroom ketchup is an excellent subsitute.
Anchovy essence may be omitted from recipes.

THE LEAF SYMBOL NEXT TO A RECIPE INDICATES THAT IT IS SUITABLE FOR VEGANS.

CONTENTS

SOUPS & STARTERS

Tantalising appetizers range from traditional favourites – including
soups that could be served either before a main course or on their own
as a light and wholesome meal – to more exotic dishes for elegant dinners.

Vegetable Stock

Use this versatile stock as the basis for all good soups and sauces. If you've an extra large saucepan, or preserving pan, why not make double the quantity and freeze several batches?

MAKES 2.25 LITRES/4 PINTS/10 CUPS
2 leeks, roughly chopped
3 sticks celery, roughly chopped
1 large onion, with skin, chopped
2 pieces fresh root ginger, chopped
3 garlic cloves, unpeeled
1 yellow pepper, seeded and chopped
1 parsnip, chopped
mushroom stalks
tomato peelings
45 ml/3 tbsp light soy sauce
3 bay leaves
bundle of parsley stalks
3 sprigs of fresh thyme
1 sprig of fresh rosemary
10 ml/2 tsp salt
ground black pepper
3.5 litres/6 pints/15 cups cold water

1 Put all the ingredients into a very large saucepan or a small preserving pan.

2 Bring slowly to the boil, then lower the heat and simmer for 30 minutes, stirring from time to time.

3 Allow the liquid and vegetables to cool. Strain, discard the vegetables and the stock is ready to use. Alternatively, chill or freeze the stock and keep it to use as required.

CRISP CROÛTONS

Easy to make and simple to store, these croûtons add a delightful touch to fresh homemade soups.

They are also an ideal way of using up stale bread. Speciality bread such as Ciabatta or baguettes can be thinly sliced to make the nicest, crunchiest croûtons, but everyday sliced loaves can be cut into interesting shapes for fun entertaining. Use a good quality, flavourless oil such as sunflower or groundnut, or for a fuller flavour brush with extra virgin olive oil. Alternatively, you could use a flavoured oil such as one with garlic and herbs or chilli.

Preheat the oven to 200°C/ 400°F/Gas 6. Place the croûtons on a baking sheet, brush with your chosen oil than bake for about 15 minutes until golden and crisp. They crisp up further as they cool. Store them in an airtight container for up to a week. Reheat in a warm oven if liked, before serving.

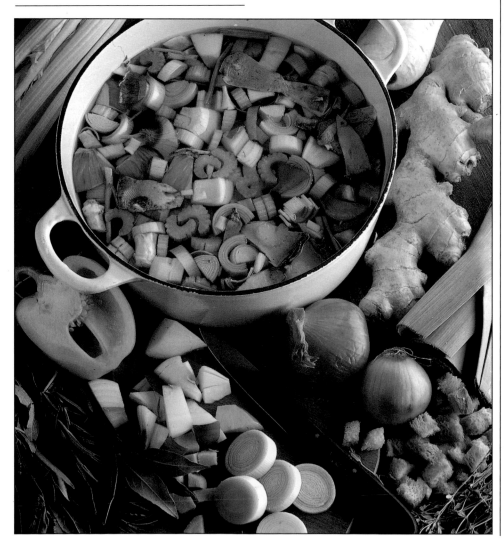

Sweetcorn and Potato Chowder

This hearty and substantial American soup is high in both fibre and flavour. It's wonderful served with thick crusty bread and topped with melted Cheddar cheese.

SERVES 4
1 onion, chopped
1 garlic clove, crushed
1 medium size potato, chopped
2 sticks celery, sliced
1 small green pepper, seeded, halved and
   sliced
30 ml/2 tbsp sunflower oil
25 g/1 oz/2 tbsp butter
600 ml/1 pint/2½ cups stock or water
salt and ground black pepper
300 ml/½ pint/1¼ cups milk
1 × 200 g/7 oz can butter beans
1 × 300 g/11 oz can sweetcorn kernels
good pinch dried sage

1 Put the onion, garlic, potato, celery and green pepper into a large saucepan with the oil and butter.

2 Heat the ingredients until sizzling then turn the heat down to low. Cover and sweat the vegetables gently for 10 minutes, shaking the pan occasionally.

3 Pour in the stock or water, season to taste and bring to the boil. Turn down the heat, cover and simmer gently for about 15 minutes.

4 Add the milk, beans and sweetcorn – including their liquors – and the sage. Simmer again for 5 minutes. Check the seasoning and serve hot.

All the Reds Soup

Vibrant in colour and taste, this soup is quickly made. Use a red onion – if you can find one – it will enhance the final appearance.

SERVES 4–6
1 red pepper, seeded and chopped
1 onion, chopped
1 garlic clove, crushed
30 ml/2 tbsp olive oil
1 × 400 g/14 oz can chopped tomatoes
1 litre/1¾ pints/4 cups stock
30 ml/2 tbsp long grain rice
30 ml/2 tbsp Worcestershire sauce
1 × 200 g/7 oz can red kidney beans
5 ml/1 tsp dried oregano
5 ml/1 tsp sugar
salt and ground black pepper
 fresh parsley, chopped, and Cheddar
  cheese, grated, to garnish

1 Put the pepper, onion, garlic and oil into a large saucepan. Heat until sizzling then turn down to low. Cover and cook gently for 5 minutes.

2 Add the rest of the ingredients, except the garnishes, and bring to a boil. Stir well, then simmer – covered – for 15 minutes. Check the seasoning, garnish and serve hot. Omit the Cheddar cheese for a vegan soup.

Chinese Tofu and Lettuce Soup

This light, clear soup is brimming full of nourishing tasty pieces. Ideally, make this in a wok with the home-made vegetable stock.

SERVES 4
30 ml/2 tbsp groundnut or sunflower oil
200 g/7 oz smoked or marinated tofu,
  cubed
3 spring onions, sliced diagonally
2 garlic cloves, cut in thin strips
1 carrot, thinly sliced in rounds
1 litre/2 pints/5 cups stock
30 ml/2 tbsp soy sauce
15 ml/1 tbsp dry sherry or vermouth
5 ml/1 tsp sugar
115 g/4 oz Cos or Romaine lettuce,
  shredded
salt and ground black pepper

1 Heat the oil in a wok, then stir-fry the tofu cubes until browned. Drain and set aside on kitchen paper towel.

2 In the same oil, stir-fry the onions, garlic and carrot for 2 minutes. Pour in the stock, soy sauce and sherry or vermouth and sugar.

Spiced Indian Cauliflower Soup

Light and tasty, this creamy, mildly spicy soup is multi-purpose. It makes a wonderful warming first course, an appetizing quick meal and – when served chilled – is delicious for any summer menu.

SERVES 4–6
1 large potato, peeled and diced
1 small cauliflower, chopped
1 onion, chopped
15 ml/1 tbsp sunflower oil
1 garlic clove, crushed
15 ml/1 tbsp fresh ginger, grated
10 ml/2 tsp ground turmeric
5 ml/1 tsp cumin seeds
5 ml/1 tsp black mustard seeds
10 ml/2 tsp ground coriander
1 litre/1¾ pints/4 cups vegetable stock
300 ml/½ pint/1¼ cups natural yogurt
salt and ground black pepper
fresh coriander or parsley, to garnish

1 Put the potato, cauliflower and onion into a large saucepan with the oil and 45 ml/3 tbsp water. Heat until hot and bubbling, then cover and turn the heat down. Continue cooking the mixture for about 10 minutes.

2 Add the garlic, ginger and spices. Stir well and cook for another 2 minutes, stirring occasionally. Pour in the stock and season well. Bring to a boil, then cover and simmer for about 20 minutes. Stir in the yogurt, season well and garnish with coriander or parsley.

Winter Warmer Soup

Simmer a selection of popular winter root vegetables together for a warming and satisfying soup. Its creamy taste comes from adding crème frâiche just before serving.

SERVES 6
3 medium carrots, chopped
1 large potato, chopped
1 large parsnip, chopped
1 large turnip or small swede, chopped
1 onion, chopped
30 ml/2 tbsp sunflower oil
25 g/1 oz/2 tbsp butter
1.5 litres/2½ pints/6 cups water
salt and ground black pepper
1 piece fresh root ginger, peeled and grated
300 ml/½ pint/1¼ cups milk
45 ml/3 tbsp crème frâiche, fromage frais or natural yogurt
30 ml/2 tbsp fresh dill, chopped

1 Put the carrots, potato, parsnip, turnip or swede and onion into a large saucepan with the oil and butter. Fry lightly, then cover and sweat the vegetables on a very low heat for 15 minutes, shaking the pan occasionally.

2 Pour in the water, bring to a boil and season well. Cover and simmer for 20 minutes until the vegetables are soft.

3 Strain the vegetables, reserving the stock, add the ginger and purée in a food processor or blender until smooth.

4 Return the purée and stock to the pan. Add the milk and stir while the soup gently reheats.

5 Remove from the heat, stir in the crème frâiche, fromage frais or yogurt plus the dill, lemon juice and extra seasoning, if necessary. Reheat the soup, if you wish, but do not allow it to boil as you do so, or it may curdle.

Cream of Mushroom Soup

Homemade mushroom soup is quite, quite different from canned or packet soups. Add a few shiitake mushrooms (which are more readily available) to give your soup a richer flavour:

SERVES 4–6
450 g/1 lb open cup mushrooms, sliced
115 g/4 oz shiitake mushrooms, sliced
45 ml/3 tbsp sunflower oil
1 onion, chopped
1 stick celery, chopped
1.2 litres/2 pints/5 cups stock or water
30 ml/2 tbsp soy sauce
50 g/2 oz/¼ cup long grain rice
salt and ground black pepper
300 ml/½ pint/1¼ cups milk
fresh parsley, chopped, or almond flakes, to garnish

1 Put all the mushrooms into a large saucepan with the oil, onion and celery. Heat until sizzling, then cover and simmer for about 10 minutes, shaking the pan occasionally.

2 Add the stock or water, soy sauce, rice and seasoning. Bring to a boil then cover and simmer gently for 20 minutes until the vegetables and rice are soft.

3 Strain the vegetables, reserving the stock, and purée until smooth in a food processor or blender. Return the vegetables and reserved stock to the pan.

4 Stir in the milk, reheat until boiling and taste for seasoning. Serve hot sprinkled with a little chopped parsley and a few almond flakes.

Classic Minestrone

This famous Italian soup has been much imitated around the world – with varying results. The homemade version is a delicious revelation and mouth-wateringly healthy with pasta, beans and fresh vegetables.

SERVES 4
1 large leek, thinly sliced
2 carrots, chopped
1 courgette, thinly sliced
115 g/4 oz whole green beans, halved
2 sticks celery, thinly sliced
45 ml/3 tbsp olive oil
1.5 litres/2½ pints/6¼ cups stock or water
1 × 400 g/14 oz can chopped tomatoes
15 ml/1 tbsp fresh basil, chopped
5 ml/1 tsp fresh thyme leaves, chopped
   or 2.5 ml/½ tsp dried thyme
salt and ground black pepper
1 × 400 g/14 oz can cannellini or kidney
   beans
50 g/2 oz/⅓ cup small pasta shapes or
   macaroni
fresh Parmesan cheese, finely grated, to
   garnish (optional)
fresh parsley, chopped, to garnish

1 Put all the fresh vegetables into a large saucepan with the olive oil. Heat until sizzling then cover, lower the heat and sweat the vegetables for 15 minutes, shaking the pan occasionally.

2 Add the stock or water, tomatoes, herbs and seasoning. Bring to the boil, replace the lid and simmer gently for about 30 minutes.

3 Add the beans and their liquor together with the pasta, and simmer for a further 10 minutes. Check the seasoning and serve hot sprinkled with the Parmesan cheese (if used) and parsley.

COOK'S TIP

Minestrone is also delicious served cold on a hot summer's day. In fact the flavour improves if made a day or two ahead and stored in the refrigerator. It can also be frozen and reheated.

Mediterranean Vegetables with Tahini

Wonderfully colourful, this starter is easily prepared in advance. For an *al fresco* meal, why not grill the vegetables on a barbecue? Tahini is a paste made from sesame seeds.

SERVES 4
2 peppers, red, green or yellow, seeded and quartered
2 courgettes, halved lengthways
2 small aubergines, degorged and halved lengthways
1 fennel bulb, quartered
olive oil
salt and ground black pepper
115 g/4 oz Greek Halloumi cheese, sliced
TAHINI CREAM
225 g/8 oz/1 cup tahini paste
1 garlic cloves, crushed
30 ml/2 tbsp olive oil
30 ml/2 tbsp fresh lemon juice
120 ml/4 fl oz/½ cup cold water

1 Preheat the grill or barbecue until hot. Brush the vegetables with the oil and grill until just browned, turning once. (If the peppers blacken, don't worry. The skins can be peeled off.) Cook the vegetables until just softened.

2 Place the vegetables in a shallow dish and season. Allow to cool. Meanwhile, brush the cheese slices with oil and grill these on both sides until just charred. Remove them with a palette knife.

3 To make the tahini cream, place all the ingredients, except the water, in a food processor or blender. Whizz for a few seconds to mix, then, with the motor still running, pour in the water and blend until smooth.

4 Serve the vegetables and cheese on a platter and trickle over the cream. Delicious served with warm pitta or naan breads.

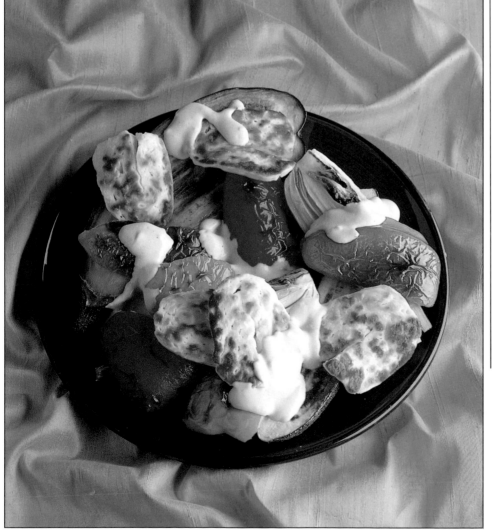

Imam Bayildi

Legend has it that a Muslim holy man – the Imam – was so overwhelmed by this dish that he fainted in sheer delight! Translated, Imam Bayildi means 'The Imam fainted'.

SERVES 4
2 medium aubergines, degorged (see Cook's Tip) and halved lengthways
salt
60 ml/4 tbsp olive oil
2 large onions, sliced thinly
2 garlic cloves, crushed
1 green pepper, seeded and sliced
1 × 400 g/14 oz can chopped tomatoes
30 g/1½ oz sugar
5 ml/1 tsp ground coriander
ground black pepper
30 ml/2 tbsp fresh coriander or parsley, chopped

1 Using a sharp knife, slash the flesh of the aubergines a few times. Sprinkle with salt and place in a colander for about half an hour. Rinse well and pat dry.

2 Gently fry the aubergines, cut side down, in the oil for 5 minutes, then drain and place in a shallow ovenproof dish.

3 In the same pan gently fry the onions, garlic and green pepper, adding extra oil if necessary. Cook for about 10 minutes, until the vegetables have softened.

4 Add the tomatoes, sugar, ground coriander and seasoning and cook for about 5 minutes until the mixture is reduced. Stir in the chopped coriander or parsley.

5 Spoon this mixture on top of the aubergines. Preheat the oven to 190° C/ 375° F/Gas 5, cover and bake for about 30–35 minutes. When cooked, cool, then chill. Serve cold with crusty bread.

COOK'S TIP

To degorge aubergines: sprinkle cut slices with salt and allow the juices that form to drain away in a colander. After 30 minutes or so, rinse well and pat dry. Degorged aubergines are less bitter and easier to cook.

Tricolour Salad

This can be a simple starter if served on individual salad plates, or part of a light buffet meal laid out on a platter. When lightly salted, tomatoes make their own flavoursome dressing with their natural juices.

SERVES 4–6
1 small red onion, sliced thinly
6 large full-flavoured tomatoes
extra virgin olive oil, to sprinkle
50 g/2 oz/small bunch rocket or
   watercress, roughly chopped
salt and ground black pepper
175 g/6 oz Mozzarella cheese, thinly sliced
   or grated
30 ml/2 tbsp pine nuts (optional)

1 Soak the onion slices in a bowl of cold water for 30 minutes, then drain and pat dry. Skin the tomatoes by slashing and dipping briefly in boiling water. Remove the core and slice the flesh.

2 Slice the tomatoes and arrange half on a large platter, or divide them between small plates.

3 Sprinkle liberally with olive oil then layer with the chopped rocket or cress, and soaked onion slices, seasoning well. Add in the cheese, sprinkling over more oil and seasoning as you go.

4 Repeat with the remaining tomato slices, salad leaves, cheese and oil.

5 Season well to finish and complete with some oil and a good scattering of pine nuts. Cover the salad and chill for at least 2 hours before serving.

Guacamole Salsa in Red Leaves

This lovely, light summery starter looks so attractive arranged in cups of radicchio leaves. Serve with chunks of warm garlic bread.

SERVES 4
2 tomatoes, skinned and chopped
15 ml/1 tbsp grated onion
1 garlic clove, crushed
1 green chilli, halved, seeded and chopped
2 ripe avocadoes
30 ml/2 tbsp olive oil
2.5 ml/½ tsp ground cumin
30 ml/2 tbsp fresh coriander or parsley, chopped
juice of 1 lime
salt and ground black pepper
leaves from radicchio lettuce

1 Using a sharp knife, slash a small cross on the top of the tomatoes, then dip them briefly in a bowl of boiling water. The skins will slip off easily. Remove the core and chop the flesh.

2 Put the tomato flesh into a bowl together with the onion, garlic and chopped chilli. Halve the avocadoes, remove the stones then scoop the flesh into the bowl, mashing it with a fork.

3 Add the remaining ingredients, except for the radicchio leaves, and mix well together, seasoning to taste.

4 Lay the radicchio leaves on a platter and spoon in the salsa. Serve immediately as avocadoes go black when exposed to the air.

COOK'S TIP

Take care when cutting chillies. The juice can sting, so be careful not to rub your eyes until you have washed your hands.

Tempura Vegetables with Dipping Sauce

A Japanese favourite, these are thinly sliced, fresh vegetables fried in a light crispy batter and served with a small bowl of flavoured soy sauce. For the best results, serve these immediately so the batter remains crisp. Tempura also makes a delicious party piece.

SERVES 4–6
1 medium courgette, sliced in thin sticks
1 red pepper, seeded and cut in wedges
3 large mushrooms, quartered
1 fennel bulb, cut in wedges with root attached
½ medium aubergine, thinly sliced
oil, for deep frying
SAUCE
45 ml/3 tbsp soy sauce
15 ml/1 tbsp medium dry sherry
5 ml/1 tsp sesame seed oil
few shreds fresh ginger or spring onion
BATTER
1 egg
115 g/4 oz/1 cup plain flour
175 ml/6 fl oz/¾ cup cold water
salt and ground black pepper

1 Prepare all the vegetables and lay them out on a tray, together with sheets of kitchen paper towel for draining the vegetables after cooking.

2 Mix the sauce ingredients together by whisking them in a jug or shaking them together in a sealed jar. Pour into a bowl.

3 Half fill a deep frying pan with oil and preheat to a temperature of about 190°C/375°F. Quickly whisk the batter ingredients together but don't overbeat them. It doesn't matter if the batter is a little lumpy.

4 Fry the vegetables in stages by dipping a few quickly into the batter and lowering into the hot oil in a wire basket. Fry for just a minute until golden brown and crisp. Drain on the paper towel.

5 Repeat until all the vegetables are fried. Keep those you have cooked, uncovered, in a warm oven while you fry the rest. Serve the vegetables on a large platter alongside the dipping sauce.

COOK'S TIP

Successful deep frying can be quite tricky and a bit hazardous. First, never leave the pan of oil unattended while the heat is turned on. If you have to leave the stove, then turn the oil off. The oil will drop in temperature during cooking so keep re-heating it between batches.

Sweetcorn Blinis with Dill Cream

A mouth-watering and unusual starter, these blinis are also suitable for a cocktail buffet. Ideally make them an hour or two before you serve them, although the batter will stand for longer.

SERVES 6–8
75 g/3 oz/¾ cup plain flour
75 g/3 oz/⅔ cup wholemeal flour
250 ml/8 fl oz/1 cup buttermilk
4 small eggs, beaten
2.5 ml/½ tsp salt
2.5 ml/½ tsp baking powder
25 g/1 oz/2 tbsp butter, melted
good pinch bicarbonate of soda
15 ml/1 tbsp hot water
1 × 200 g/7 oz can sweetcorn kernels, drained
oil, for the griddle
DILL CREAM
200 g/7 oz crème frâiche
30 ml/2 tbsp fresh dill, chopped
30 ml/2 tbsp fresh chives, chopped
salt and ground black pepper

1 Mix the two flours and buttermilk together until completely smooth. Cover and leave to chill for about 8 hours in the refrigerator.

2 Beat in the eggs, salt, baking powder and butter. Mix the bicarbonate with the hot water and add this too, along with the sweetcorn kernels.

3 Heat a griddle or heavy based frying pan until quite hot. Brush with a little oil and drop spoonfuls of the blinis mixture on to it. The mixture should start to sizzle immediately.

4 Cook until holes appear on the top and the mixture looks almost set. Using a palette knife flip the blinis over and cook briefly. Stack the blinis under a clean tea towel while you make the rest.

5 To make the cream, simply blend the crème frâiche with the herbs and seasoning. Serve the blinis with a few spoonfuls of cream and garnished with sliced radishes and herbs.

LIGHT LUNCHES & SUPPERS

For tempting lunches that are not too filling and tasty television suppers,
experiment with these glorious recipes, from those that include protein-rich
ingredients such as tofu to irresistible cheese and pasta dishes.

Mushroom and Chilli Carbonara

For a richer mushroom flavour, use a small pack of dried Italian porcini mushrooms in this quick eggy sauce, and for an extra spicy zing, toss in some chilli flakes too.

SERVES 4

1 × 15 g/½ oz pack dried porcini
  mushrooms
300 ml/½ pint/1¼ cups hot water
225 g/8 oz spaghetti
1 garlic clove, crushed
25 g/1 oz/2 tbsp butter
15 ml/1 tbsp olive oil
225 g/8 oz button or chestnut
  mushrooms, sliced
5 ml/1 tsp dried chilli flakes
2 eggs
300 ml/½ pint/1¼ cups single cream
salt and ground black pepper
fresh Parmesan cheese, grated, and
  parsley, chopped, to serve

1 Soak the dried mushrooms in the hot water for 15 minutes, drain and reserve the liquor.

2 Boil the spaghetti according to the instructions on the packet in salted water. Drain and rinse in cold water.

3 In a large saucepan, lightly sauté the garlic with the butter and oil for half a minute then add the mushrooms, including the soaked porcini ones, and the dried chilli flakes, and stir well. Cook for about 2 minutes, stirring a few times.

4 Pour in the reserved mushroom stock and boil to reduce slightly.

5 Beat the eggs with the cream and season well. Return the cooked spaghetti to the pan and toss in the eggs and cream. Reheat, without boiling, and serve hot sprinkled with Parmesan cheese and chopped parsley.

VARIATION

Instead of mushrooms, try using either finely sliced and sautéed leeks or perhaps coarsely shredded lettuce with peas. If chilli flakes are too hot and spicy for you, then try the delicious alternative of skinned and chopped tomatoes with torn, fresh basil leaves.

Tagliatelle with 'Hit-the-pan' Salsa

It is possible to make a hot filling meal within just fifteen minutes with this quick-cook salsa sauce. If you don't have time to peel the tomatoes, then don't bother.

SERVES 2
115 g/4 oz tagliatelle
45 ml/3 tbsp olive oil, preferably extra
  virgin
3 large tomatoes
1 garlic clove, crushed
4 spring onions, sliced
1 green chilli, halved, seeded and sliced
juice of 1 orange (optional)
30 ml/2 tbsp fresh parsley, chopped
salt and ground black pepper
cheese, grated, to garnish (optional)

1 Boil the tagliatelle in plenty of salted water until it is *al dente*. Drain and toss in a little of the oil. Season well.

2 Skin the tomatoes by dipping them briefly in a bowl of boiling water. The skins should slip off easily. Chop the tomatoes roughly.

3 Heat the remaining oil until it is quite hot and stir-fry the garlic, onions and chilli for a minute. The pan should sizzle.

4 Add the tomatoes, orange juice (if using) and parsley. Season well and stir in the tagliatelle to reheat. Serve with the grated cheese (if used).

COOK'S TIP

You could use any pasta shape for this recipe. It would be particularly good with large rigatoni or linguini, or as a sauce for fresh ravioli or tortellini.

Cheesy Bubble and Squeak

This London breakfast dish is enjoying something of a revival. Originally made on Mondays with leftover potatoes and cabbage from the Sunday lunch, it is suitable for any light meal occasion. For breakfast, serve the bubble and squeak with eggs, grilled tomatoes and mushrooms.

SERVES 4
about 450 g/1 lb/3 cups mashed potato
about 225 g/8 oz cooked cabbage or kale, shredded
1 egg, beaten
115 g/4 oz Cheddar cheese, grated
fresh nutmeg, grated
salt and ground black pepper
plain flour, for coating
oil, for frying

1 Mix the potatoes with the cabbage or kale, egg, cheese, nutmeg and seasoning. Divide and shape into eight patties.

2 Chill for an hour or so, if possible, as this enables the mixture to become firm and makes it easier to fry. Toss the patties in the flour. Heat about 1 cm/½ in of oil in a frying pan until it is quite hot.

3 Carefully slide the patties into the oil and fry on each side for about 3 minutes until golden and crisp. Drain on kitchen paper towel and serve hot and crisp.

Cheese and Chutney Toasties

Quick cheese on toast can be made quite memorable with a few tasty additions. Serve these scrumptious toasties with a simple salad.

SERVES 4
4 slices wholemeal bread, thickly sliced
butter or low fat spread
115 g/4 oz Cheddar cheese, grated
5 ml/1 tsp dried thyme
ground black pepper
30 ml/2 tbsp chutney or relish

1 Toast the bread slices lightly on each side then spread sparingly with butter or low fat spread.

2 Mix the cheese and thyme together and season with pepper.

3 Spread the chutney or relish on the toast and divide the cheese between the four slices.

4 Return to the grill and cook until browned and bubbling. Cut into halves, diagonally, and serve with salad.

Risotto Primavera

Real Italian risottos should be creamy and full of flavour. They are best made freshly and do need frequent stirring, but this can be done in between other jobs in the kitchen. For best results use a quality Arborio rice which has a good *al dente* bite.

SERVES 4

1 litre/1¾ pints/4 cups hot stock, preferably homemade
1 red onion, chopped
2 garlic cloves, crushed
30 ml/2 tbsp olive oil
25 g/1 oz/2 tbsp butter
225 g/8 oz/1¼ cups risotto rice (do not rinse)
45 ml/3 tbsp dry white wine
115 g/4 oz asparagus spears or green beans, sliced and blanched
2 young carrots, sliced and blanched
50 g/2 oz baby button mushrooms
salt and ground black pepper
50 g/2 oz Pecorino or Parmesan cheese, grated

1 It is important to follow the steps for making real risotto so that you achieve the right texture. First, heat the stock in a saucepan to simmering.

2 Next to it, in a large saucepan, sauté the onion and garlic in the oil and butter for 3 minutes.

3 Stir in the rice making sure each grain is coated well in the oil, then stir in the wine. Allow to reduce down and spoon in two ladles of hot stock, stirring continuously.

4 Allow this to bubble down then add more stock and stir again. Continue like this, ladling in the stock and stirring frequently for up to 20 minutes, by which time the rice will have swelled greatly.

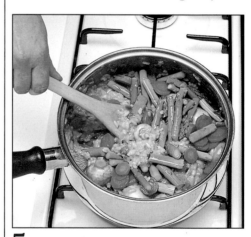

5 Mix in the asparagus or beans, carrots and mushrooms, seasoning well, and cook for a minute or two more. Serve immediately in bowls with a scattering of grated cheese.

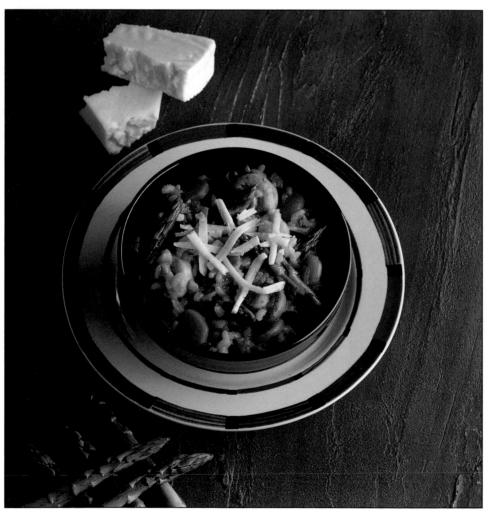

VARIATION

If you have any left-over risotto, shape it into small balls and then coat in beaten egg and dried breadcrumbs. Chill for 30 minutes before deep frying in hot oil until golden and crisp.

Kitchiri

This is the Indian original which inspired the classic breakfast dish known as kedgeree. Made with basmati rice and small tasty lentils this will make an ample supper or brunch dish.

SERVES 4

115 g/4 oz/1 cup Indian masoor
    dhal or Continental green lentils
1 onion, chopped
1 garlic clove, crushed
50 g/2 oz/4 tbsp vegetarian ghee or butter
30 ml/2 tbsp sunflower oil
225 g/8 oz/1¼ cups easy-cook basmati rice
10 ml/2 tsp ground coriander
10 ml/2 tsp cumin seeds
2 cloves
3 cardamom pods
2 bay leaves
1 stick cinnamon
1 litre/1¾ pints/4 cups stock
30 ml/2 tbsp tomato purée
salt and ground black pepper
45 ml/3 tbsp fresh coriander or parsley,
    chopped

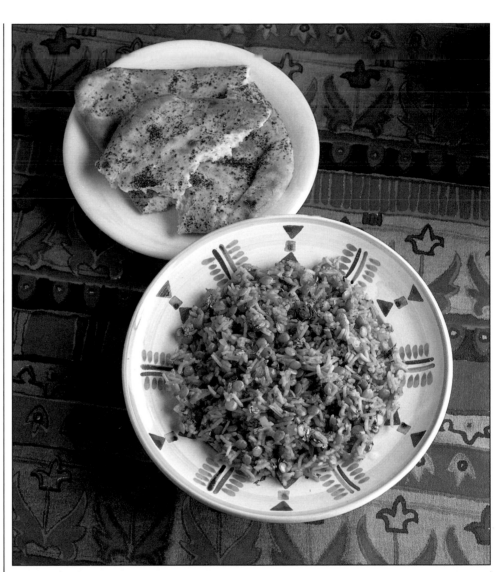

1 Cover the dhal or lentils with boiling water and soak for 30 minutes. Drain and boil in fresh water for 10 minutes. Drain once more and set aside.

2 Fry the onion and garlic in the ghee or butter and oil in a large saucepan for about 5 minutes.

3 Add the rice, stir well to coat the grains in the ghee or butter and oil, then stir in the spices. Cook gently for a minute or so.

4 Add the lentils, stock, tomato purée and seasoning. Bring to the boil, then cover and simmer for 20 minutes until the stock is absorbed and the lentils and rice are just soft. Stir in the coriander or parsley and check the seasoning. Remove the cinnamon stick and bay leaf.

Baked Potatoes and Three Fillings

Potatoes baked in their jackets and packed with a variety of fillings make an excellent and nourishing meal. Although they have been cooked here in a conventional oven, potatoes can be baked more quickly and just as successfully in a microwave.

4 medium size baking potatoes
olive oil, for greasing
sea salt, to serve

1 Preheat the oven to 200°C/400°F/ Gas 6. Score the potatoes with a cross and rub all over with the olive oil.

2 Place on a baking sheet and cook for 45–60 minutes until a knife inserted into the centres indicates they are cooked.

3 Cut the potatoes open along the score lines and push up the flesh from the base with your fingers. Season with salt and fill with your chosen filling.

EACH FILLING IS FOR FOUR POTATOES

RED BEAN FILLING
1 × 425 g/15 oz can red kidney beans
200 g/7 oz low fat cheese or cream cheese
30 ml/2 tbsp mild chilli sauce
5 ml/1 tsp ground cumin

Red Bean – drain the beans, heat in a pan or microwave and stir in the cream cheese, chilli sauce and cumin.

SOY VEGETABLES FILLING
2 leeks, thinly sliced
2 carrots, cut in sticks
1 courgette, thinly sliced
115 g/4 oz baby sweetcorn, halved
45 ml/3 tbsp groundnut or sunflower oil
115 g/4 oz button mushrooms, sliced
45 ml/3 tbsp soy sauce
30 ml/2 tbsp dry sherry or vermouth
15 ml/1 tbsp sesame oil
sesame seeds, to sprinkle

Soy Vegetables – stir-fry the leeks, carrots, courgettes and baby corn in the oil for about 2 minutes then add the mushrooms and cook for a further minute. Mix together the soy sauce, sherry and sesame oil and pour over the vegetables. Heat until bubbling then scatter over the sesame seeds.

CHEESY CREAMED CORN FILLING
1 × 425 g/15 oz can creamed corn
115 g/4 oz cheese, grated
5 ml/1 tsp dried mixed herbs

Cheesy creamed corn – heat the corn, add the cheese and mixed herbs.

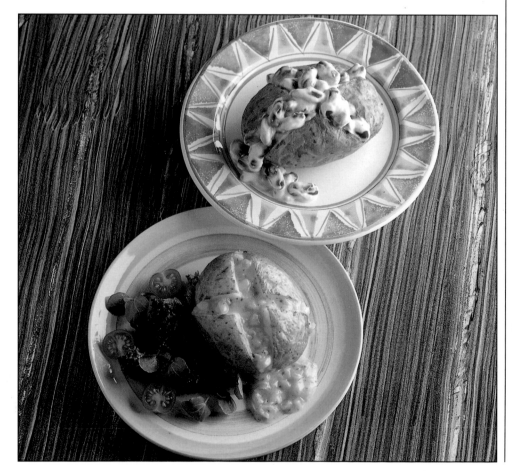

Peanut Butter Fingers

Children will love these crispy, tasty croquettes. Make up a batch and freeze some ready for whenever there are young tummies to fill!

MAKES 12
1 kg/2 lb potatoes
1 large onion, chopped
2 large peppers, red or green, chopped
3 carrots, coarsely grated
45 ml/3 tbsp sunflower oil
2 courgettes, coarsely grated
115 g/4 oz mushrooms, chopped
15 ml/1 tbsp dried mixed herbs
115 g/4 oz mature Cheddar cheese, grated
75 g/3 oz/½ cup crunchy peanut butter
salt and ground black pepper
2 eggs, beaten
about 50 g/2 oz/½ cup dried breadcrumbs
45 ml/3 tbsp dried Parmesan cheese
oil, for deep frying

1 Boil the potatoes until tender, then drain well and mash. Set aside.

2 Fry the onion, peppers and carrots gently in the oil for about 5 minutes then add the courgettes and mushrooms. Cook for 5 minutes more.

3 Mix the potato with the dried mixed herbs, grated cheese and peanut butter. Season, allow to cool for 30 minutes, then stir in one of the eggs.

4 Spread out on a large plate, cool and chill, then divide into 12 portions and shape. Dip your hands in cold water if the mixture sticks.

5 Put the second egg in a bowl and dip the potato fingers into it first, then into the crumbs and Parmesan cheese until coated evenly. Return to the fridge to set.

6 Heat oil in a deep fat frier to 190°C/375°F then fry the fingers in batches for about 3 minutes until golden. Drain well on kitchen paper towel. Serve hot.

COOK'S TIP

To reheat, thaw for about 1 hour, then grill or oven bake at 190°C/375°F/Gas 5 for 15 minutes.

Pasta Salade Tiède

Boil a pan of pasta shapes and toss with vinaigrette dressing and some freshly prepared salad vegetables and you have the basis for a delicious warm salad.

SERVES 2
115 g/4 oz pasta shapes, e.g. shells
45 ml/3 tbsp vinaigrette dressing
3 sun-dried tomatoes in oil, snipped
2 spring onions, sliced
25 g/1 oz/2 or 3 sprigs watercress or rocket, chopped
¼ cucumber, halved, seeded and sliced
salt and ground black pepper
about 40 g/1½ oz Pecorino cheese, coarsely grated

1 Boil the pasta according to the instructions on the packet. Drain and toss in the dressing.

2 Mix in the tomatoes, onions, cress or rocket and cucumber. Season to taste.

3 Divide between two plates and sprinkle over the cheese. Eat at room temperature, if possible.

Penne with 'Can Can' Sauce

The quality of canned pulses and tomatoes is so good that it is possible to transform them into a very fresh tasting pasta sauce in minutes. Again, choose whatever pasta you like.

SERVES 3–4
225 g/8 oz penne pasta
1 onion, sliced
1 red pepper, seeded and sliced
30 ml/2 tbsp olive oil
1 × 400 g/14 oz can chopped tomatoes
1 × 425 g/15 oz can chick peas
30 ml/2 tbsp dry vermouth (optional)
5 ml/1 tsp dried oregano
1 large bay leaf
30 ml/2 tbsp capers
salt and ground black pepper

1 Boil the pasta as instructed on the package, then drain. In a saucepan, gently fry the onion and pepper in the oil for about 5 minutes, stirring occasionally, until softened.

2 Add the tomatoes, chick peas with their liquor, vermouth (if liked), herbs and capers.

3 Season and bring to a boil then simmer for about 10 minutes. Remove the bay leaf and mix in the pasta, reheat and serve hot.

Tofu and Crunchy Vegetables

High protein, wonder food tofu is nicest if marinated lightly before cooking. If you use the smoked tofu, it's even tastier. For successful stir-frying, make sure all your ingredients are prepared first.

SERVES 4
2 × 225 g/8 oz cartons smoked tofu, cubed
45 ml/3 tbsp soy sauce
30 ml/2 tbsp dry sherry or vermouth
15 ml/1 tbsp sesame oil
45 ml/3 tbsp groundnut or sunflower oil
2 leeks, thinly sliced
2 carrots, cut in sticks
1 large courgette, thinly sliced
115 g/4 oz baby sweetcorn, halved
115 g/4 oz button or shiitake mushrooms, sliced
15 ml/1 tbsp sesame seeds
1 packet of egg noodles, cooked

1 Marinate the tofu in the soy sauce, sherry or vermouth and sesame oil for at least half an hour. Drain and reserve the marinade.

2 Heat the groundnut or sunflower oil in a wok and stir-fry the tofu cubes until browned all over. Remove and reserve.

3 Stir-fry the leeks, carrots, courgette and baby corn, stirring and tossing for about 2 minutes. Add the mushrooms and cook for a further minute.

4 Return the tofu to the wok and pour in the marinade. Heat until bubbling, then scatter over the sesame seeds.

5 Serve as soon as possible with the hot cooked noodles, dressed in a little sesame oil, if liked.

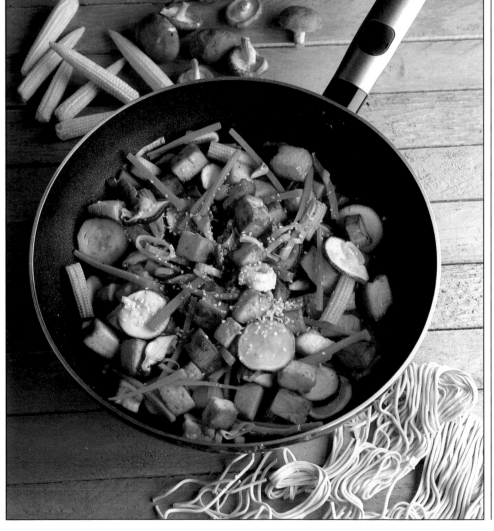

VARIATION

Tofu is also excellent marinated and skewered, then lightly grilled. Push the tofu off the skewers into pockets of pitta bread. Fill with lemon-dressed salad and serve with a final trickle of tahini cream.

Egg Foo Yung

A great way of turning a bowl of leftover cooked rice into a meal for four, this Oriental dish is tasty and full of texture. Use bought beansprouts or grow your own – it's easy and fun.

SERVES 4

salt and ground black pepper
3 eggs, beaten
good pinch five spice powder (optional)
45 ml/3 tbsp groundnut or sunflower oil
4 spring onions, sliced
1 garlic clove, crushed
1 small green pepper, seeded and
  chopped
115 g/4 oz fresh bean sprouts
225 g/8 oz/3 cups cooked white rice
45 ml/3 tbsp light soy sauce
15 ml/1 tbsp sesame oil

1 Season the eggs and beat in the five spice powder, if using.

2 In a wok or large frying pan, heat one tablespoon of the oil and when quite hot, pour in the egg.

3 Cook rather like an omelette, pulling the mixture away from the sides and allowing the rest to slip underneath.

4 Cook the egg until firm then tip out. Chop the 'omelette' into small strips.

5 Heat the remaining oil and stir-fry the onion, garlic, pepper and bean sprouts for about 2 minutes, stirring and tossing continuously.

6 Mix in the rice and heat thoroughly, stirring well. Add the soy sauce and sesame oil then return the egg and mix in well. Serve immediately, piping hot.

Light Ratatouille

This lightly cooked medley of fresh vegetables is cooked with simple poached eggs and served topped with crisply fried breadcrumbs.

SERVES 4
45 ml/3 tbsp olive oil
50 g/2 oz/1 cup fresh white breadcrumbs
1 yellow or red pepper, seeded and thinly sliced
2 garlic cloves, crushed
2 leeks, thinly sliced
2 courgettes, thinly sliced
2 tomatoes, skinned and sliced
5 ml/1 tsp dried rosemary, crushed
4 eggs
salt and ground black pepper

1 Heat half the oil in a shallow fireproof dish (or frying pan with a lid) and fry the breadcrumbs until they are golden and crisp. Drain on kitchen paper towel.

2 Add the remaining oil and fry the pepper, garlic and leeks in the same pan for about 10 minutes until softened.

3 Add the courgettes, tomatoes and rosemary and cook for a further 5 minutes. Season well.

4 Using the back of a spoon, make four wells in the vegetable mixture and break an egg into each one. Lightly season the eggs then cover and cook on a gentle heat for about 3 minutes until they are just set.

5 Sprinkle over the crisp breadcrumbs and serve immediately, piping hot.

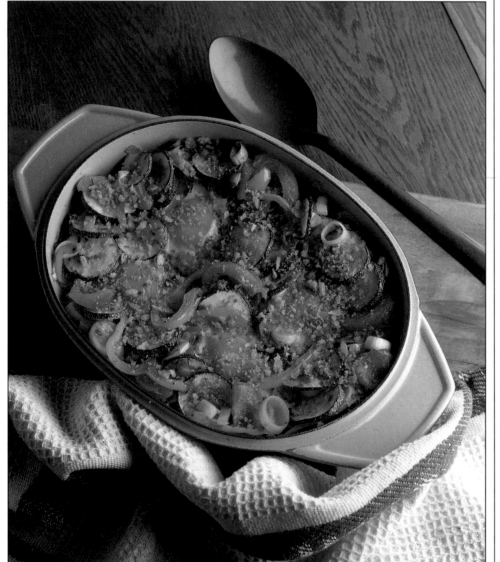

Macaroni Soufflé

This is generally a great favourite with children, and is rather like a light and fluffy macaroni cheese. Make sure you serve a soufflé immediately it is cooked or it will sink dramatically.

SERVES 3–4
75 g/3 oz short cut macaroni
melted butter, to coat
25 g/1 oz/3 tbsp dried breadcrumbs
50 g/2 oz/4 tbsp butter
5 ml/1 tsp ground paprika
40 g/1½ oz/⅓ cup plain flour
300 ml/½ pint/1¼ cups milk
75 g/3 oz Cheddar or Gruyère cheese, grated
50 g/2 oz Parmesan cheese, grated
salt and ground black pepper
3 eggs, separated

1 Boil the macaroni according to the instructions on the pack. Drain well and then set aside. Preheat the oven to 150°C/300°F/Gas 2.

2 Brush the insides of a 1.2 litre/2 pint soufflé dish with melted butter then coat evenly with the breadcrumbs, shaking out any excess.

3 Put the butter, paprika, flour and milk into a saucepan and bring to the boil slowly, whisking it constantly until it is smooth and thick.

4 Simmer the sauce for a minute, then take off the heat and stir in the cheeses until they melt. Season well and mix with the macaroni.

5 Beat in the egg yolks. Whisk the egg whites until they form soft peaks and spoon a quarter into the sauce mixture, beating it gently to loosen it up.

6 Using a large metal spoon, carefully fold in the rest of the egg whites and transfer to the prepared soufflé dish.

7 Bake in the centre of the oven for about 40–45 minutes until the soufflé has risen and is golden brown. The middle should wobble very slightly and the soufflé should be lightly creamy inside.

Cowboy Hot Pot

A great dish to serve as a children's main meal, which adults will enjoy too – if they are allowed to join the posse. You can use any vegetable mixture you like; although beans are a must for every self-respecting cowboy!

SERVES 4–6
1 onion, sliced
1 red pepper, sliced
1 sweet potato or 2 carrots, chopped
45 ml/3 tbsp sunflower oil
115 g/4 oz green beans, chopped
1 × 400 g/14 oz can baked beans
1 × 200 g/7 oz can sweet corn
15 ml/1 tbsp tomato purée
5 ml/1 tsp barbecue spice seasoning
115 g/4 oz cheese (preferably smoked), cubed
450 g/1 lb potatoes, thinly sliced
25 g/1 oz/2 tbsp butter, melted
salt and ground black pepper

1 Fry the onion, pepper and sweet potato or carrots gently in the oil until softened but not browned.

2 Add the green beans, baked beans, sweetcorn (and liquor), tomato purée and barbecue spice seasoning. Bring to a boil then simmer for 5 minutes.

3 Transfer the vegetables to a shallow ovenproof dish and then scatter with the cubed cheese.

4 Cover the vegetable and cheese mixture with the sliced potato, brush with butter, season and bake at 190°C/375°F/Gas 5 for 30–40 minutes until golden brown on top and the potato is cooked.

Stir-fry Rice and Vegetables

If you have some left-over cooked rice and a few vegetables lurking at the bottom of the refrigerator, then you've got the basis for this quick and tasty meal.

SERVES 4
½ cucumber
2 spring onions, sliced
1 garlic clove, crushed
2 carrots, thinly sliced
1 small red or yellow pepper, seeded and sliced
45 ml/3 tbsp sunflower or groundnut oil
¼ small green cabbage, shredded
225 g/8 oz/4 cups cooked long grain rice
30 ml/2 tbsp light soy sauce
15 ml/1 tbsp sesame oil
salt and ground black pepper
fresh parsley or coriander, chopped (optional)
115 g/4 oz unsalted cashew nuts, almonds or peanuts

1 Halve the cucumber lengthways and scoop out the seeds with a teaspoon. Slice the flesh diagonally. Set aside.

2 In a wok or large frying pan, stir-fry the onions, garlic, carrots and pepper in the oil for about 3 minutes until they are just soft.

3 Add the cabbage and cucumber and fry for another minute or two until the leaves begin to just wilt. Mix in the rice, soy sauce, sesame oil and seasoning. Reheat the mixture thoroughly, stirring and tossing all the time.

4 Add the herbs, if using, and nuts. Check the seasoning and serve piping hot.

Pepper and Potato Tortilla

A great favourite with my family, tortilla is rather like a thick omelette or pastry-less quiche. Traditionally a Spanish dish, it is best eaten cold in chunky wedges. Tortilla makes ideal picnicking food. Use a hard Spanish cheese, like Mahon, or a goats' cheese, if you can, although mature Cheddar makes a good substitute.

SERVES 4
2 medium size potatoes
45 ml/3 tbsp olive oil
1 large onion, thinly sliced
2 garlic cloves, crushed
2 peppers, one green and one red, thinly sliced
6 eggs, beaten
115 g/4 oz mature cheese, grated
salt and ground black pepper

1 Do not peel the potatoes, but wash them thoroughly. Par-boil them as they are for about 10 minutes, then drain and slice them thickly. Switch on the grill so that it has time to warm up while you prepare the tortilla.

2 In a large non-stick or well seasoned frying pan, heat the oil and fry the onion, garlic and peppers on a moderate heat for 5 minutes until softened.

3 Add the potatoes and continue frying, stirring occasionally until the potatoes are completely cooked and the vegetables are soft. Add a little extra oil if the pan seems rather dry.

4 Pour in half the eggs, then sprinkle over half the cheese then the rest of the egg, seasoning as you go. Finish with a layer of cheese.

5 Continue to cook on a low heat, without stirring, half covering the pan with a lid to help set the eggs.

6 When the mixture is firm, flash the pan under the hot grill to just lightly seal the top. Leave the tortilla in the pan to cool. This helps it firm up further and makes it easier to turn out.

VARIATION

You can add any sliced and lightly cooked vegetable, such as mushrooms, courgettes or broccoli, to this tortilla dish instead of peppers. Cooked pasta or brown rice are both excellent alternatives too.

Cauliflower and Egg Cheese

No need to make a traditional béchamel sauce for this country classic. A quick all-in-one sauce can be made in minutes while a small pack of soup croûtons gives the dish a delicious crunchy topping.

SERVES 4

1 medium size cauliflower, broken in
  florets
1 medium onion, sliced
2 eggs, hard boiled, peeled and chopped
40 g/1½ oz/3 tbsp wholemeal flour
5 ml/1 tsp mild curry powder
25 g/1 oz/2 tbsp sunflower margarine or
  low fat spread
450 ml/¾ pint/2 cups milk
2.5 ml/½ tsp dried thyme
salt and ground black pepper
115 g/4 oz mature cheese, grated
small packet of soup croûtons

1 Boil the cauliflower and onion in enough salted water to cover until they are just tender. Be careful not to overcook them. Drain well.

2 Arrange the cauliflower and onion in a shallow ovenproof dish and scatter over the chopped egg.

3 Put the flour, curry powder, fat and milk in a saucepan all together. Bring slowly to the boil, stirring well until thickened and smooth. Stir in the thyme and seasoning and allow the sauce to simmer for a minute or two. Remove the pan from the heat and stir in about three quarters of the cheese.

4 Pour the sauce over the cauliflower, scatter over the croûtons and sprinkle with the remaining cheese. Brown under a hot grill until golden and serve. Delicious with thick crusty bread.

Quorn with Ginger, Chilli and Leeks

Quorn is a newly-developed, versatile mycoprotein food which easily absorbs different flavours and retains a good firm texture. This makes it ideal for stir-frying. It is available in most supermarkets.

SERVES 4
225 g/8 oz Quorn cubes
45 ml/3 tbsp soy sauce
30 ml/2 tbsp dry sherry or vermouth
10 ml/2 tsp clear honey
150 ml/¼ pint/⅔ cup stock
10 ml/2 tsp cornflour
45 ml/3 tbsp sunflower or groundnut oil
3 leeks, thinly sliced
1 red chilli, seeded and sliced
2.5 cm/1 in piece fresh root ginger, peeled and shredded
salt and ground black pepper

1 Toss the Quorn in the soy sauce and sherry or vermouth until well coated and leave to marinate for about 30 minutes.

2 Strain the Quorn from the marinade and reserve the juices in a jug. Mix the marinade with the honey, stock and cornflour to make a paste.

3 Heat the oil in a wok or large frying pan and when hot, stir-fry the Quorn until it is crisp on the outside. Remove the Quorn and set aside.

4 Reheat the oil and stir-fry the leeks, chilli and ginger for about 2 minutes until they are just soft. Season lightly.

5 Return the Quorn to the pan, together with the marinade, and stir well until the liquid is thick and glossy. Serve hot with rice or egg noodles.

Chinese Potatoes with Chilli Beans 🍃

East meets West. An American style dish with a Chinese flavour — the sauce is particularly tasty. Try it as a quick supper dish when you fancy a meal with a little zing!

SERVES 4
4 medium potatoes, cut in thick chunks
3 spring onions, sliced
1 large fresh chilli, seeded and sliced
30 ml/2 tbsp sunflower or groundnut oil
2 garlic cloves, crushed
1 × 400 g/14 oz can red kidney beans, drained
30 ml/2 tbsp soy sauce
15 ml/1 tbsp sesame oil
TO SERVE
salt and ground black pepper
15 ml/1 tbsp sesame seeds
fresh coriander or parsley, chopped, to garnish

1 Boil the potatoes until they are just tender. Take care not to overcook them. Drain and reserve.

2 In a large frying pan or wok, stir-fry the onions and chilli in the oil for about 1 minute then add the garlic and fry for a few seconds longer.

3 Add the potatoes, stirring well, then the beans and finally the soy sauce and sesame oil.

4 Season to taste and cook the vegetables until they are well heated through. Sprinkle with the sesame seeds and the coriander or parsley.

Pitta Pizzas

Pitta breads make very good bases for quick thin and crispy pizzas, and they are easy to eat with your hands too. The perfect speedy snack.

SERVES 4
BASIC PIZZAS
4 pitta breads, ideally wholemeal
small jar of pasta sauce
225 g/8 oz Mozzarella cheese, sliced or grated
dried oregano or thyme, to sprinkle
salt and ground black pepper
EXTRA TOPPINGS – CHOOSE FROM
1 small red onion, thinly sliced and lightly fried
mushrooms, sliced and fried
1 × 200 g/7 oz can sweetcorn, drained
jalapeno chillis, sliced
black or green olives, stoned and sliced
capers, drained

1 Prepare two or three toppings of your choice for the pizzas.

2 Preheat the grill and lightly toast the pitta breads on each side.

3 Spread pasta sauce on each pitta, right to the edge. This prevents the edges of the pitta from burning.

4 Arrange cheese slices or grated cheese on top of each pitta and sprinkle with herbs and seasoning.

5 Add the toppings of your choice and then grill the pizzas for about 5–8 minutes until they are golden brown and bubbling. Serve immediately.

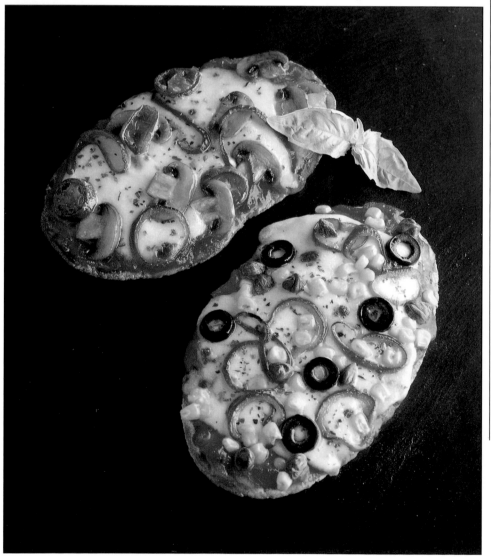

Tagliatelle with Spinach and Soy Garlic Cheese

It's wonderful to mix ingredients from different cuisines and produce a delicious dish as a result. Italian pasta and spinach combine with Chinese soy and French garlic cream cheese to create this wonderful rich and mouth-watering dish.

SERVES 4

225 g/8 oz tagliatelle, preferably mixed colours
225 g/8 oz fresh leaf spinach
30 ml/2 tbsp light soy sauce
75 g/3 oz garlic and herb cheese
45 ml/3 tbsp milk
salt and ground black pepper

1 Boil the tagliatelle according to the instructions on the pack and drain. Return the pasta to the pan.

2 Meanwhile blanch the spinach in a tiny amount of water until just wilted, then drain very well, squeezing dry with the back of a wooden spoon. Chop roughly with kitchen scissors.

3 Return the spinach to its pan and stir in the soy sauce, garlic and herb cheese and milk. Bring slowly to a boil, stirring until smooth. Season to taste.

4 When the sauce is ready, pour it over the pasta. Toss the pasta and sauce together well and serve hot.

Aduki Bean Burgers

Although not quick to make, these burgers are a delicious alternative to shop-bought ones; so it is worth making up several batches for the freezer. Make sure you use an ordinary long-grain brown rice and not a quick-cook variety.

MAKES 12
200 g/7 oz/1 cup brown rice
1 onion, chopped
2 garlic cloves, crushed
30 ml/2 tbsp sunflower oil
50 g/2 oz/4 tbsp butter
1 small green pepper, seeded and chopped
1 carrot, coarsely grated
1 × 400 g/14 oz can aduki beans, drained (or 125 g/4 oz dried weight, soaked and cooked)
1 egg, beaten
125 g/4 oz mature cheese, grated
5 ml/1 tsp dried thyme
50 g/2 oz/½ cup roasted hazelnuts or toasted flaked almonds
salt and ground black pepper
wholemeal flour or cornmeal, for coating
oil, for deep frying

1 Cook the rice according to the instructions on the pack, allowing it to slightly overcook so that it is softer. Strain the rice and transfer it to a large bowl.

2 Fry the onion and garlic in the oil and butter together with the green pepper and carrot for about 10 minutes until the vegetables are softened.

3 Mix this vegetable mixture into the rice, together with the aduki beans, egg, cheese, thyme, nuts or almonds and plenty of seasoning. Chill until quite firm.

4 Shape into 12 patties, using wet hands if the mixture sticks. Coat the patties in flour or cornmeal and set aside.

5 Heat 1 cm/½ in oil in a large, shallow frying pan and fry the burgers in batches until browned on each side, about five minutes in total. Remove and drain on kitchen paper. Eat some burgers freshly cooked, and freeze the rest for later. Serve in buns with salad and relish.

COOK'S TIP

To freeze the burgers, cool them after cooking, then open freeze them before wrapping and bagging. Use within six weeks. Cook from frozen by baking in a pre-heated moderately hot oven for 20–25 minutes.

Courgette Quiche

If possible, use a hard goats' cheese for this flan as its flavour complements the courgettes nicely. Bake the pastry base blind for a crisp crust.

SERVES 6
PASTRY
115 g/4 oz/scant 1 cup wholemeal flour
115 g/4 oz/1 cup plain flour
115 g/4 oz/½ cup sunflower margarine
FILLING
1 red onion, thinly sliced
30 ml/2 tbsp olive oil
2 large courgettes, sliced
175 g/6 oz cheese, grated
30 ml/2 tbsp fresh basil, chopped
3 eggs, beaten
300 ml/½ pint/1¼ cups milk
salt and ground black pepper

1 Preheat the oven to 200°C/400°F/ Gas 6. Mix the flours together and rub in the margarine until it resembles crumbs then mix to a firm dough with cold water.

2 Roll out the pastry and use it to line a 23–25 cm/9–10 in flan tin, ideally at least 2.5 cm/1 in deep. Prick the base, chill for 30 minutes then fill with paper or foil and baking beans.

3 Bake the pastry case blind on a baking sheet for 20 minutes uncovering it for the last 5 minutes so that it can crisp up.

4 Meanwhile, sweat the onion in the oil for 5 minutes, until it is soft. Add the courgettes and fry for another 5 minutes.

5 Spoon the onion and courgettes into the pastry case. Scatter over most of the cheese and all of the basil.

6 Beat together the eggs, milk and seasoning and pour over the filling. Top with the remaining cheese.

7 Turn the oven down to 180°C/350°F/ Gas 4 and return the flan for about 40 minutes until risen and just firm to the touch in the centre. Allow to cool slightly before serving.

MAIN COURSES

Create healthy and satisfying meals that make the most of the wonderful variety of herbs and spices, as well as nutritious ingredients such as lentils, rice and vegetables.

Arabian Spinach

Stir-fry spinach with onions and spices, then mix in a can of chick peas and you have a delicious family main course meal in next to no time.

SERVES 4
1 onion, sliced
30 ml/2 tbsp olive or sunflower oil
2 garlic cloves, crushed
400 g/14 oz spinach, washed and shredded
5 ml/1 tsp cumin seeds
1 × 425 g/15 oz can chick peas, drained
knob of butter
salt and ground black pepper

1 In a large frying pan or wok, fry the onion in the oil for about 5 minutes until softened. Add the garlic and cumin seeds, then fry for another minute.

2 Add the spinach, in stages, stirring it until the leaves begin to wilt. Fresh spinach condenses down dramatically on cooking and it *will* all fit into the pan.

3 Stir in the chick peas, butter and seasoning. Reheat until just bubbling, then serve hot. Drain off any pan juices, if you like, but this dish is rather nice served slightly saucy.

Vegetable Medley with Lentil Bolognese

Instead of a white or cheese sauce, it makes a nice change to top a selection of lightly steamed vegetables with a healthy and delicious lentil sauce.

SERVES 6
1 small cauliflower, in florets
225 g/8 oz broccoli florets
2 leeks, thickly sliced
225 g/8 oz Brussels sprouts, halved if large
Lentil Bolognese Sauce

1 Make up the sauce and keep warm.

2 Place all the vegetables in a steamer over a pan of boiling water and cook for 8–10 minutes until just tender.

3 Drain and place in a shallow serving dish. Spoon the sauce on top, stirring slightly to mix. Serve hot.

Falafels

Made with ground chick peas, herbs and spices, falafels are a Middle Eastern street food normally served tucked into warm pitta breads with scoopfuls of salad. They are absolutely delicious served with tahini cream or dollops of natural yogurt.

MAKES 8
1 × 425 g/15 oz can chick peas, drained
1 garlic clove, crushed
30 ml/2 tbsp fresh parsley, chopped
30 ml/2 tbsp fresh coriander, chopped
15 ml/1 tbsp fresh mint, chopped
5 ml/1 tsp cumin seeds
30 ml/2 tbsp fresh breadcrumbs
5 ml/1 tsp salt
ground black pepper
oil, for deep frying

1 Grind the chick peas in a food processor until they are just smooth, then mix them with all the other ingredients until you have a thick, creamy paste. Add pepper to taste.

2 Using wet hands, shape the chick pea mixture into 8 rounds and chill for 30 minutes so that they become firm.

3 Meanwhile, heat about 5 mm/¼ in of oil in a shallow frying pan and fry the falafels a few at a time. Cook each one for about 8 minutes, turning the falafels carefully just once.

4 Drain the falafels on kitchen paper towel and fry the rest in batches, reheating the oil in between. Serve tucked inside warm pitta breads with sliced salad, tomatoes and tahini cream or yogurt.

COOK'S TIP

Falafels can be made in batches and frozen. Allow them to cool, spread out on wire cooling racks and open freeze until solid. Tip into a freezer-proof plastic container. To reheat, bake in a moderate oven for 10–15 minutes.

Caribbean Rice and Peas

A great family favourite in West Indian culture, this dish is not only very tasty, but nutritionally well balanced too. Serve with the gravy sauce and slices of fried aubergine.

SERVES 4
225 g/8 oz/1¼ cups easy-cook long grain rice
115 g/4 oz/¾ cup dried gunga peas or red kidney beans, soaked and cooked but still firm
750 ml/1¼ pints/3⅔ cups water
50 g/2 oz creamed coconut, chopped
5 ml/1 tsp dried thyme or 15 ml/1 tbsp fresh thyme leaves
1 small onion stuck with 6 whole cloves
salt and ground black pepper

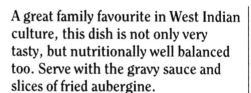

1 Put the rice and peas or kidney beans into a large saucepan with the water, coconut, thyme, onion and seasoning.

2 Bring to the boil, stirring until the coconut melts then cover and simmer gently for 20 minutes.

3 Remove the lid and allow to cook uncovered for 5 minutes to reduce down any excess liquid. Remove from the heat and stir occasionally to separate the grains. The rice should be quite dry.

Greek Stuffed Vegetables

Vegetables such as peppers make wonderful containers for savoury fillings. Instead of sticking to one type of vegetable, follow the Greeks' example and serve an interesting selection. Thick, creamy Greek yogurt is the ideal accompaniment.

SERVES 3–6
1 medium aubergine
1 large green pepper
2 large tomatoes
1 large onion, chopped
2 garlic cloves, crushed
45 ml/3 tbsp olive oil
200 g/7 oz/1 cup brown rice
600 ml/1 pint/2½ cups stock
75 g/3 oz/¾ cup pine nuts
50 g/2 oz/⅓ cup currants
salt and ground black pepper
45 ml/3 tbsp fresh dill, chopped
45 ml/3 tbsp fresh parsley, chopped
15 ml/1 tbsp fresh mint, chopped
extra olive oil, to sprinkle
natural Greek yogurt, to serve
fresh sprigs of dill

1 Halve the aubergine, scoop out the flesh with a sharp knife and chop finely. Salt the insides and leave to drain upside down for 20 minutes while you prepare the other ingredients.

2 Halve the pepper, seed and core. Cut the tops from the tomatoes, scoop out the insides and chop roughly along with the tomato tops.

3 Fry the onion, garlic and chopped aubergine in the oil for 10 minutes, then stir in the rice and cook for 2 minutes.

4 Add the tomato flesh, stock, pine nuts, currants and seasoning. Bring to the boil, cover and simmer for 15 minutes then stir in the fresh herbs.

5 Blanch the aubergine and green pepper halves in boiling water for about 3 minutes, then drain them upside down.

6 Spoon the rice filling into all six vegetable 'containers' and place on a lightly greased ovenproof shallow dish.

7 Heat the oven to 190°C/375°F/Gas 5, drizzle over some olive oil and bake the vegetables for 25–30 minutes. Serve hot, topped with spoonfuls of natural yogurt and dill sprigs.

Red Onion and Courgette Pizza

It's easy to make a homemade pizza using one of the new fast-action yeasts. You can either add the traditional cheese and tomato topping or try something different, such as the one described here.

SERVES 4
350 g/12 oz/3 cups plain flour
1 sachet fast action/easy blend yeast
10 ml/2 tsp salt
lukewarm water to mix
TOPPING
2 red onions, thinly sliced
60 ml/4 tbsp olive oil
2 courgettes, thinly sliced
salt and ground black pepper
fresh nutmeg, grated
about 115 g/4 oz semi-soft goats' cheese
6 sun-dried tomatoes in oil, snipped
dried oregano
extra olive oil, to sprinkle

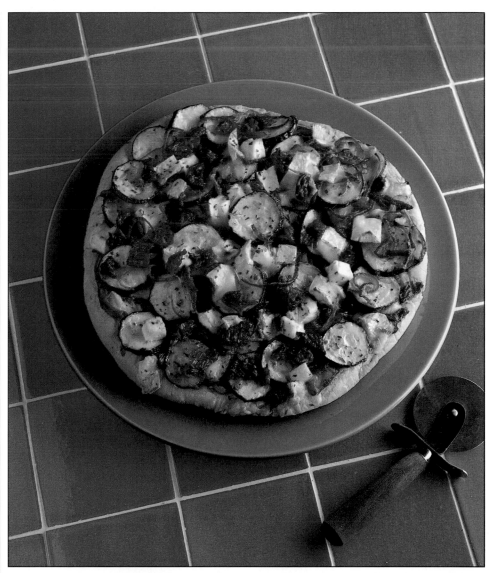

1 Preheat the oven to 200°C/400°F/ Gas 6. Mix the flour, yeast and salt together, then mix to a firm dough with warm water. How much depends on the flour, but start with 150 ml/¼ pint.

2 Knead the dough for about 5 minutes until it is smooth and elastic then roll it out to a large circle and place on a lightly greased baking sheet.

3 Set the base aside somewhere warm to rise slightly while you make the topping.

4 Gently fry the onions in half the oil for 5 minutes then add the courgettes and fry for a further 2 minutes. Season and add nutmeg to taste.

5 Spread the pizza base with fried vegetable mixture and dot with the cheese, tomatoes and oregano. Sprinkle over the rest of the olive oil and bake for 12–15 minutes until golden and crisp.

Shepherdess Pie 🌿

A no-meat version of the timeless classic, this dish also has no dairy products in it, so it is suitable for vegans. However, you can serve it with confidence to anyone wanting a hearty meal.

SERVES 6–8
1 kg/2 lb potatoes
45 ml/3 tbsp extra virgin olive oil
salt and ground black pepper
1 large onion, chopped
1 green pepper, chopped
2 carrots, coarsely grated
2 garlic cloves
45 ml/3 tbsp sunflower oil or margarine
115 g/4 oz mushrooms, chopped
2 × 400 g/14 oz cans aduki beans, drained
600 ml/1 pint/2½ cups stock
5 ml/1 tsp vegetable yeast extract
2 bay leaves
5 ml/1 tsp dried mixed herbs
dried breadcrumbs or chopped nuts, to sprinkle

1 Boil the potatoes in the skins until tender, then drain, reserving a little of the water to moisten them.

2 Mash well, mixing in the olive oil and seasoning until you have a smooth purée. (Potatoes are easier to peel when boiled in their skins. This also preserves vitamins.)

3 Gently fry the onion, pepper, carrots and garlic in the sunflower oil or margarine for about 5 minutes until they are soft. Preheat the grill.

4 Stir in the mushrooms and beans and cook for a further 2 minutes, then add the stock, yeast extract, bay leaves and mixed herbs. Simmer for 15 minutes.

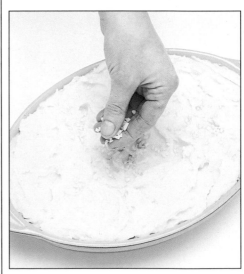

5 Remove the bay leaves and empty the vegetables into a shallow ovenproof dish. Spoon on the potatoes in dollops and sprinkle over the crumbs or nuts. Grill until golden brown.

Magnificent Marrow 🥬

At autumn time, marrows – with their wonderful green and cream stripes – look so attractive and tempting. They make delicious, inexpensive main courses, just right for a satisfying family Sunday lunch.

SERVES 4–6
250 g/8 oz/3 cups pasta shells
1.5–1.75 kg/3–4 lb marrow
1 onion, chopped
1 pepper, seeded and chopped
15 ml/1 tbsp fresh root ginger, grated
2 garlic cloves, crushed
45 ml/3 tbsp sunflower oil
4 large tomatoes, skinned and chopped
salt and ground black pepper
50 g/2 oz/½ cup pine nuts
15 ml/1 tbsp fresh basil, chopped
cheese, grated, to serve (optional)

1 Preheat the oven to 190°C/375°F/ Gas 5. Boil the pasta according to the instructions on the pack, slightly overcooking it so it is just a little soft. Drain and reserve.

2 Cut the marrow in half lengthways and scoop out the seeds. These can be discarded. Use a small sharp knife and tablespoon to scoop out the marrow flesh. Chop the flesh roughly.

3 Gently fry the onion, pepper, ginger and garlic in the oil for 5 minutes then add the marrow flesh, tomatoes and seasoning. Cover and cook for 10–12 minutes until the vegetables are soft.

4 Add to the pan the pasta, pine nuts and basil, stir well and set aside.

5 Meanwhile, place the marrow halves in a roasting pan, season lightly and pour a little water around the marrow, taking care it does not spill inside. Cover with foil and bake for 15 minutes.

6 Remove the foil, discard the water and fill the shells with the vegetable mixture. Recover with foil and return to the oven for a further 20–25 minutes.

7 If you wish, serve this dish topped with grated cheese. The marrow can either be served cut into sections or scooped out of the 'shell'.

Turnip and Chick Pea Cobbler

A good mid-week meal with an attractive savoury scone topping. Use a star shape cutter for the topping.

SERVES 4–6
1 onion, sliced
2 carrots, chopped
3 medium size turnips, chopped
1 small sweet potato or swede, chopped
2 celery sticks, sliced thinly
45 ml/3 tbsp sunflower oil
2.5 ml/½ tsp ground coriander
2.5 ml/½ tsp dried mixed herbs
1 × 425 g/15 oz can chopped tomatoes
1 × 400 g/14 oz can chick peas
1 vegetable stock cube
salt and ground black pepper
TOPPING
225 g/8 oz/2 cups self-raising flour
5 ml/1 tsp baking powder
50 g/2 oz/4 tbsp margarine
45 ml/3 tbsp sunflower seeds
30 ml/2 tbsp Parmesan cheese, grated
150 ml/¼ pint/⅔ cup milk

1 Fry all the vegetables in the oil for about 10 minutes until they are soft. Add the coriander, herbs, tomatoes, chick peas with their liquor and stock cube. Season well and simmer for 20 minutes.

2 Pour the vegetables into a shallow casserole dish while you make the topping. Preheat the oven to 190°C/375°F/Gas 5.

3 Mix together the flour and baking powder then rub in the margarine until it resembles fine crumbs. Stir in the seeds and Parmesan cheese. Add the milk and mix to a firm dough.

4 Lightly roll out the topping to a thickness of 1 cm/½ in and stamp out star shapes or rounds, or simply cut it into small squares.

5 Place the shapes on top of the vegetable mixture and brush with a little extra milk. Bake for 12–15 minutes until risen and golden brown. Serve hot with green, leafy vegetables.

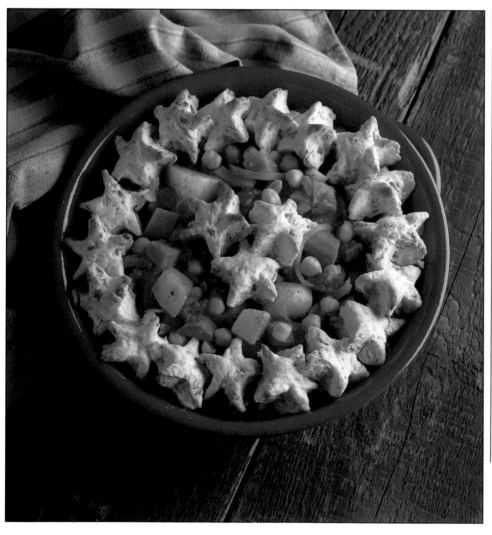

Tangy Fricassé

Vegetables in a light tangy sauce and covered with a crispy crumb topping make a simple and easy main course to serve with crusty bread and salad.

SERVES 4
4 courgettes, sliced
115 g/4 oz green beans, sliced
4 large tomatoes, skinned and sliced
1 onion, sliced
50 g/2 oz/4 tbsp butter or sunflower
  margarine
40 g/1½ oz/⅓ cup plain flour
10 ml/2 tsp coarse grain mustard
450 ml/¾ pint/2 cups milk
150 ml/¼ pint/⅔ cup natural yogurt
5 ml/1 tsp dried thyme
115 g/4 oz mature cheese, grated
salt and ground black pepper
60 ml/4 tbsp fresh wholemeal
  breadcrumbs tossed with 15 ml/1 tbsp
  sunflower oil

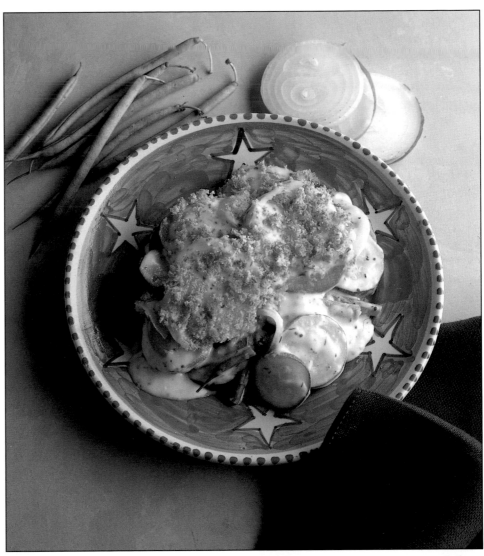

1 Blanch the courgettes and beans in a small amount of boiling water for just 5 minutes then drain and arrange in a shallow ovenproof dish.

2 Arrange all but three slices of tomato on top. Put the onion into a saucepan with the butter or margarine and fry gently for 5 minutes.

3 Stir in the flour and mustard, cook for a minute then add the milk gradually until the sauce has thickened. Simmer for a further 2 minutes.

4 Remove the pan from the heat, add the yogurt, thyme and cheese, stirring until melted. Season to taste. Reheat gently if you wish, but do not allow the sauce to boil or it will curdle.

5 Pour the sauce over the vegetables and scatter the breadcrumbs on top. Brown under a preheated grill until golden and crisp, taking care not to let them burn. Garnish with the reserved tomato slices if desired.

Pistachio Pilaff in a Spinach Crown

Saffron and ginger are traditional rice spices and even more delicious when mixed with fresh pistachio nuts. This is a particularly good, light main course needing just a tomato salad for accompaniment.

SERVES 4
3 onions
60 ml/4 tbsp olive oil
2 garlic cloves, crushed
2.5 cm/1 in cube fresh root ginger, grated
1 fresh green chilli, chopped
2 carrots, coarsely grated
225 g/8 oz/1¼ cups basmati rice, rinsed
1.25 ml/¼ tsp saffron strands, crushed
450 ml/¾ pint/2 cups stock
1 cinnamon stick
5 ml/1 tsp ground coriander
salt and ground black pepper
75 g/3 oz/¼ cup fresh pistachio nuts
450 g/1 lb fresh leaf spinach
5 ml/1 tsp garam masala powder

1 Roughly chop two of the onions. Heat half the oil in a large saucepan and fry the onion with half the garlic, the ginger and the chilli for 5 minutes.

2 Mix in the carrots and rice, cook for 1 more minute and then add the saffron, stock, cinnamon and coriander. Season well. Bring to a boil, then cover and simmer gently for 10 minutes, without lifting the lid.

3 Remove from the heat and leave to stand, uncovered, for 5 minutes. Add the pistachio nuts, mixing them in with a fork. Remove the cinnamon stick and keep the rice warm.

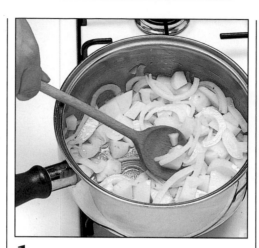

4 Thinly slice the third onion and fry in the remaining oil for about 3 minutes. Stir in the spinach. Cover and cook for another 2 minutes.

5 Add the garam masala powder. Cook until just tender, then drain and roughly chop the spinach.

6 Spoon the spinach round the edge of a round serving dish and pile the pilaff in the centre. Serve hot.

Spinach Bread and Butter Bake

Ideally use Italian ciabatta bread for this, or failing that, a French style baguette. It gives a much lighter bake.

SERVES 4–6
400 g/14 oz fresh leaf spinach
1 ciabatta loaf, thinly sliced
50 g/2 oz/4 tbsp softened butter, olive oil or low fat spread
1 red onion, thinly sliced
115 g/4 oz mushrooms, thinly sliced
30 ml/2 tbsp olive oil
5 ml/1 tsp cumin seeds
salt and ground black pepper
115 g/4 oz Gruyère or Gouda cheese, grated
3 eggs
500 ml/18 fl oz/2¼ cups milk
fresh nutmeg, grated

1 Rinse the spinach well and blanch it in the tiniest amount of water for 2 minutes. Drain well, pressing out any excess water and chop roughly.

2 Spread the bread slices thinly with the butter or low fat spread. Grease a large shallow ovenproof dish and line the base and sides with bread.

3 Fry the onion and mushrooms lightly in the oil for 5 minutes then add the cumin seeds and spinach. Season well.

4 Layer the spinach mixture with the remaining bread and half the cheese. For the top, mix everything together and sprinkle over the remaining cheese.

5 Beat the eggs with the milk, adding seasoning and nutmeg to taste. Pour slowly over the whole dish and set aside for a good hour to allow the custard to be absorbed into the bread.

6 Preheat the oven to 190°C/375°F/Gas 5. Stand the dish in a roasting pan and pour around some boiling water for a bain marie. Bake for 40–45 minutes until risen, golden brown and crispy on top.

Mushroom Puff Pasties

If possible, use the more full-flavoured chestnut or brown mushrooms for these tasty pasties.

MAKES 8
2 × 225 g/8 oz blocks frozen puff pastry, thawed
1 egg, beaten
FILLING
1 onion, chopped
1 carrot, coarsely grated
1 medium potato, coarsely grated
45 ml/3 tbsp sunflower oil
225 g/8 oz sliced mushrooms
30 ml/2 tbsp soy sauce
15 ml/1 tbsp tomato ketchup
15 ml/1 tbsp dry sherry (optional)
good pinch dried thyme
salt and ground black pepper

1 Roll out the pastry blocks until they are 6 mm/¼ in thick and cut each block into four 15 cm/6 in squares. Reserve a little pastry for decoration. Cover the rolled pastry squares and oddments and set aside in a cool place to rest.

2 Make the filling by gently frying the onion, carrot and potato in the oil for 5 minutes, then add the mushrooms, soy sauce, ketchup, sherry (if using), thyme and seasoning.

3 Cook, stirring occasionally, until the mushrooms and vegetables have softened and feel quite tender. Cool.

4 Divide the filling between the eight squares, placing it to one side across the diagonal. Brush the pastry edges with egg then fold over into triangles and press well to seal. From the pastry scraps, cut out little shapes, such as mushrooms, to decorate the pasties.

5 Crimp each pastie edge and top with the cut-out shapes. Set on two baking sheets. Preheat the oven to 200°C/400°F/ Gas 6 and in the meantime allow the pasties to rest somewhere cool.

6 Glaze the pasties with beaten egg, then bake for 15–20 minutes until golden brown and crisp.

Winter Casserole with Herb Dumplings

When the cold weather draws in, gather together a good selection of vegetables and make this comforting casserole with some hearty old-fashioned dumplings.

SERVES 6
2 potatoes
2 carrots
1 small fennel bulb
1 small swede
2 leeks
2 courgettes
50 g/2 oz/4 tbsp butter or margarine
30 ml/2 tbsp plain flour
1 × 425 g/15 oz can butter beans, with liquor
600 ml/1 pint/2½ cups stock
30 ml/2 tbsp tomato purée
1 cinnamon stick
10 ml/2 tsp ground coriander
2.5 ml/½ tsp ground ginger
2 bay leaves
salt and ground black pepper
DUMPLINGS
200 g/7 oz/1½ cups plain flour
115 g/4 oz vegetable suet, shredded, or chilled butter, grated
5 ml/1 tsp dried thyme
5 ml/1 tsp salt
120 ml/4 fl oz/½ cup milk

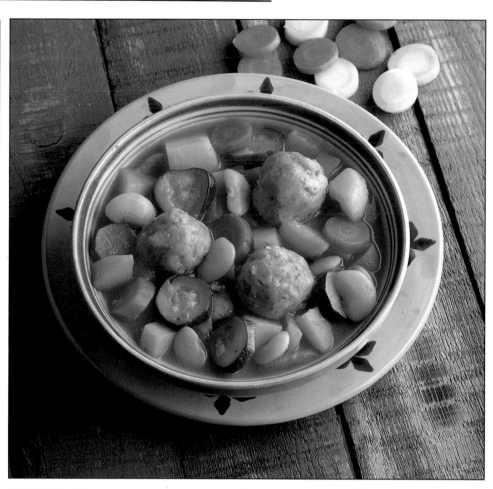

1 Cut all the vegetables into even, bite size chunks, then fry gently in the butter or margarine for about 10 minutes.

2 Stir in the flour then the liquor from the beans, the stock, tomato purée, spices, bay leaves and seasoning. Bring to the boil, stirring.

3 Cover and simmer for 10 minutes then add the beans and cook for a further 5 minutes.

4 Meanwhile, to make the dumplings, simply mix the flour, suet or butter, thyme and salt to a firm but moist dough with the milk and knead with your hands until it is smooth.

VARIATION

Try chopped walnuts and grated Parmesan or dumplings *fines herbes*. Finely chop ingredients and stir into flour.

5 Divide the dough into 12 pieces, rolling each one into a ball with your fingers. Uncover the simmering stew and then add the dumplings, allowing space between each one for expansion.

6 Replace the lid and cook on a gentle simmer for a further 15 minutes. Do not peek – or you will let out all the steam. Neither should you cook dumplings too fast, or they will break up. Remove the cinnamon stick and bay leaves before you serve this dish, steaming hot.

Lasagne Rolls

Perhaps a more elegant presentation than ordinary lasagne, but just as tasty and popular. You will need to boil 'no-need-to-cook' lasagne as it needs to be soft enough to roll!

SERVES 4
8–10 lasagne sheets
lentil bolognese (see below)
225 g/8 oz fresh leaf spinach
115 g/4 oz mushrooms, sliced
115 g/4 oz Mozzarella cheese, thinly sliced
BECHAMEL SAUCE
40 g/1½ oz/scant ½ cup plain flour
40 g/1½ oz/3 tbsp butter or margarine
600 ml/1 pint/2½ cups milk
bay leaf
salt and ground black pepper
fresh nutmeg, grated
freshly grated Parmesan or Pecorino
  cheese, to serve

Lentil Bolognese

A really useful sauce to serve with pasta, such as lasagne rolls, as a pancake stuffing or even as a protein-packed sauce for vegetables.

SERVES 6
1 onion, chopped
2 garlic cloves, crushed
2 carrots, coarsely grated
2 celery sticks, chopped
45 ml/3 tbsp olive oil
115 g/4 oz/⅔ cup red lentils
1 × 400 g/14 oz can chopped tomatoes
30 ml/2 tbsp tomato purée
450 ml/¾ pint/2 cups stock
15 ml/1 tbsp fresh marjoram, chopped, or
  5 ml/1 tsp dried marjoram
salt and ground black pepper

1 Cook lasagne sheets according to instructions on the pack, or for about 10 minutes. Drain and allow to cool.

2 Cook the spinach in the tiniest amount of water for 2 minutes then add the sliced mushrooms and cook for a further 2 minutes. Drain very well, pressing out all the excess liquor, and chop roughly.

3 Put all the bechamel ingredients into a saucepan and bring slowly to a boil, stirring continuously until the sauce is thick and smooth. Simmer for 2 minutes with the bay leaf then season well and stir in grated nutmeg to taste.

VARIATION

Needless to say, the fillings in this recipe could be any of your own choice. One of my favourites is a lightly stir-fried mixture of colourful vegetables such as peppers, courgettes, aubergines and mushrooms, topped with a cheesy béchamel as above, or with a fresh tomato sauce, which is especially good in summer.

---

4 Lay out the pasta sheets and spread with the bolognese, spinach and mushrooms and Mozzarella. Roll up each one and place in a large shallow casserole dish with the join face down.

5 Remove and discard the bay leaf and then pour the sauce over the pasta. Sprinkle over the cheese and place under a hot grill to brown.

1 In a large saucepan, gently fry the onion, garlic, carrots and celery in the oil for about 5 minutes, until they are soft.

2 Add the lentils, tomatoes, tomato purée, stock, marjoram and seasoning.

3 Bring the mixture to a boil then partially cover with a lid and simmer for 20 minutes until thick and soft. Use the bolognese as required.

Broccoli Risotto Torte

Like a Spanish omelette, this is a savoury cake served in wedges. It is good cold or hot, and needs only a salad as an accompaniment.

SERVES 6
225 g/8 oz broccoli, cut into very small florets
1 onion, chopped
2 garlic cloves, crushed
1 large yellow pepper, sliced
30 ml/2 tbsp olive oil
50 g/2 oz/4 tbsp butter
225 g/8 oz/1¼ cups risotto rice
120 ml/4 fl oz/½ cup dry white wine
1 litre/1¾ pints/4½ cups stock
salt and ground black pepper
115 g/4 oz Pecorino or Parmesan cheese, coarsely grated
4 eggs, separated
oil, for greasing
sliced tomato and chopped parsley, to garnish

1 Blanch the broccoli for 3 minutes then drain and reserve.

2 In a large saucepan, gently fry the onion, garlic and pepper in the oil and butter for 5 minutes until they are soft.

3 Stir in the rice, cook for a minute then pour in the wine. Cook, stirring the mixture until the liquid is absorbed.

4 Pour in the stock, season well, bring to the boil then lower to a simmer. Cook for 20 minutes, stirring occasionally.

5 Meanwhile, grease a 25 cm/10 in round deep cake tin and line the base with a disc of greaseproof paper. Preheat the oven to 180°C/350°F/Gas 4.

6 Stir the cheese into the rice, allow the mixture to cool for 5 minutes, then beat in the egg yolks.

7 Whisk the egg whites until they form soft peaks and carefully fold into the rice. Turn into the prepared tin and bake for about 1 hour until risen, golden brown and slightly wobbly in the centre.

8 Allow the torte to cool in the tin, then chill if serving cold. Run a knife round the edge of the tin and shake out onto a serving plate. If liked, garnish with sliced tomato and chopped parsley.

Leek and Chèvre Lasagne

An unusual and lighter than average lasagne using a soft French goats' cheese. The pasta sheets are not so chewy if boiled briefly first. If you do choose no-cook lasagne, then make more sauce to soak into the pasta.

SERVES 6
6–8 lasagne pasta sheets
salt
1 large aubergine
3 leeks, thinly sliced
30 ml/2 tbsp olive oil
2 red peppers, roasted
200 g/7 oz chèvre, broken into pieces
50 g/2 oz Pecorino or Parmesan cheese, freshly grated
SAUCE
60 g/2½ oz/½ cup plain flour
60 g/2½ oz/5 tbsp butter
900 ml/1½ pints/3¾ cups milk
2.5 ml/½ tsp ground bay leaves
fresh nutmeg, grated
ground black pepper

1 Blanch the pasta sheets in plenty of boiling water for just 2 minutes. Drain and place on a clean tea towel.

2 Lightly salt the aubergine and lay in a colander to drain for 30 minutes, then rinse and pat dry with kitchen paper.

3 Lightly fry the leeks in the oil for about 5 minutes until softened. Peel the roasted peppers and cut into strips.

4 Make the sauce: put the flour, butter and milk into a saucepan and bring to the boil, stirring constantly until it has thickened. Add the ground bay leaves, nutmeg and seasoning. Simmer for a further 2 minutes.

5 In a greased shallow casserole, layer the leeks, pasta, aubergine, chèvre and Pecorino or Parmesan. Trickle the sauce over the layers, ensuring that plenty goes in between.

6 Finish with a layer of sauce and grated cheese. Bake in the oven at 190°C/375°F/ Gas 5 for 30 minutes or until browned on top. Serve immediately.

Glamorgan Sausages

An old Welsh recipe which tastes particularly good served with creamy mashed potatoes and lightly cooked green cabbage.

SERVES 4

115 g/4 oz/2 cups fresh wholemeal breadcrumbs
150 g/6 oz mature Cheddar or Caerphilly cheese, grated
30 ml/2 tbsp leek or spring onion, finely chopped
30 ml/2 tbsp fresh parsley, chopped
15 ml/1 tbsp fresh marjoram, chopped
15 ml/1 tbsp coarse grain mustard
2 eggs, 1 separated
ground black pepper
50 g/2 oz/½ cup dried breadcrumbs
oil, for deep fat frying

1 Mix the fresh breadcrumbs with the cheese, leek or onion, parsley, marjoram, mustard, whole egg, one egg yolk and ground black pepper to taste. The mixture may appear dry at first but knead it lightly with your fingers and it will come together. Make 8 small sausage shapes.

2 Whisk the egg white until lightly frothy and put the dried breadcrumbs into a bowl. Dip the sausages first into egg white, and then coat them evenly in breadcrumbs, shaking off any excess.

3 Heat a deep fat frying pan a third full of oil and carefully fry four sausages at a time for 2 minutes each. Drain on kitchen paper towel and reheat the oil to repeat.

4 Keep the sausages warm in the oven, uncovered. Alternatively, open freeze, bag and seal, then to reheat, thaw for 1 hour and cook in a moderately hot oven for 10–15 minutes.

Brazilian Stuffed Peppers

Colourful and full of flavour, these stuffed peppers are easy to make in advance. They can be reheated quickly in a microwave oven and browned under a grill.

SERVES 4

4 peppers, halved and seeded
1 aubergine, cut in chunks
1 onion, sliced
1 garlic clove, crushed
30 ml/2 tbsp olive oil
1 × 400 g/14 oz can chopped tomatoes
5 ml/1 tsp ground coriander
salt and ground black pepper
15 ml/1 tbsp fresh basil, chopped
115 g/4 oz goats' cheese, coarsely grated
30 ml/2 tbsp dried breadcrumbs

1 Blanch the pepper halves in boiling water for 3 minutes, then drain well.

2 Sprinkle the aubergine chunks with salt, place in a colander and leave to drain for 20 minutes. Rinse and pat dry.

3 Fry the onion and garlic in the oil for 5 minutes until they are soft, then add the aubergine and cook for a further 5 minutes, stirring occasionally.

VARIATION

There are all sorts of delicious stuffings for peppers. Rice or pasta make a good base, mixed with some lightly fried onion, garlic and spices. Mixed nuts, finely chopped, can be added and a beaten egg or grated cheese helps to bind it all together. Vegans can leave out the last two ingredients.

4 Pour in the tomatoes, coriander and seasoning. Bring to the boil, then simmer for 10 minutes until the mixture is thick. Cool slightly, stir in the basil and half of the cheese.

5 Spoon into the pepper halves and place on a shallow heatproof serving dish. Sprinkle with cheese and breadcrumbs, then brown lightly under the grill. Serve with rice and salad.

Couscous-stuffed Cabbage

A whole stuffed cabbage makes a wonderful main dish, especially for a Sunday lunch. It can be made ahead and steamed when required. Cut into wedges and serve accompanied by a fresh tomato or cheese sauce or even a vegetarian gravy.

SERVES 4
1 medium size cabbage
115 g/4 oz/1 cup couscous grains
1 onion, chopped
1 small red pepper, chopped
2 garlic cloves, crushed
30 ml/2 tbsp olive oil
5 ml/1 tsp ground coriander
2.5 ml/½ tsp ground cumin
good pinch ground cinnamon
115 g/4 oz/½ cup green lentils, soaked
600 ml/1 pint/2½ cups stock
30 ml/2 tbsp tomato purée
salt and ground black pepper
30 ml/2 tbsp fresh parsley, chopped
30 ml/2 tbsp pine nuts or flaked almonds
75 g/3 oz mature Cheddar cheese, grated
1 egg, beaten

1 Cut the top quarter off the cabbage and remove any loose outer leaves. Using a small sharp knife, cut out as much of the middle as you can. Reserve a few larger leaves for later.

2 Blanch the cabbage in a pan of boiling water for 5 minutes, then drain it well, upside down.

VARIATION

You could substitute healthy brown rice for the couscous.

---

3 Steam the couscous according to the instructions on the pack, ensuring they are light and fluffy.

4 Lightly fry the onion, pepper and garlic in the oil for 5 minutes until soft then stir in the spices and cook for a further 2 minutes.

5 Add the lentils and pour in the stock and tomato purée. Bring to the boil, season and simmer for 25 minutes until the lentils are cooked.

6 Mix in the couscous, parsley, nuts or almonds, cheese and egg. Check the seasoning again. Open up the cabbage and spoon in the stuffing.

7 Blanch the leftover outer cabbage leaves and place these over the top of the stuffing, then wrap the whole thing in a sheet of buttered foil.

8 Place in a steamer over simmering water and cook for about 45 minutes. Remove from the foil and serve cut into wedges.

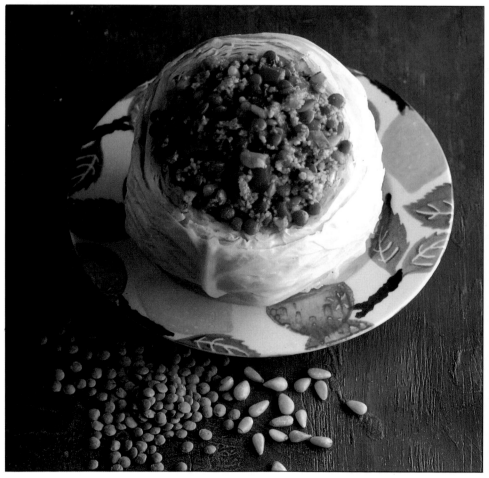

Couscous Aromatique

The cuisine of Morocco and Tunisia has many wonderful dishes using the wheat grain couscous which is steamed over simmering spicy stews. A little of the fiery harissa paste stirred in at the end adds an extra zing.

SERVES 4–6
450 g/1 lb couscous grains
60 ml/4 tbsp olive oil
1 onion, cut in chunks
2 carrots, cut in thick slices
4 baby turnips, halved
8 small new potatoes, halved
1 green pepper, cut in chunks
115 g/4 oz green beans, halved
1 small fennel bulb, sliced thickly
2.5 cm/1 in cube fresh root ginger, grated
2 garlic cloves, crushed
5 ml/1 tsp ground turmeric
15 ml/1 tbsp ground coriander
5 ml/1 tsp cumin seeds
5 ml/1 tsp ground cinnamon
45 ml/3 tbsp red lentils
1 × 400 g/14 oz can chopped tomatoes
1 litre/1¾ pints/4½ cups stock
60 ml/4 tbsp raisins
salt and ground black pepper
rind and juice of 1 lemon
harissa paste, to serve (optional)

1 Cover the couscous with cold water and soak for 10 minutes. Drain and spread out on a tray for 20 minutes, stirring it occasionally with your fingers.

2 Meanwhile, in a large saucepan, heat the oil and fry the vegetables for about 10 minutes, stirring from time to time.

3 Add the ginger, garlic and spices, stir well and cook for 2 minutes. Pour in the lentils, tomatoes, stock and raisins, and add seasoning.

4 Bring to a boil, then turn down to a simmer. By this time the couscous should be ready for steaming. Place in a steamer and fit this on top of the stew.

5 Cover and steam gently for about 20 minutes. The grains should be swollen and soft. Fork through and season well. Spoon into a serving dish.

6 Add the lemon rind and juice to the stew and check the seasoning. If liked, add harissa paste to taste; it is quite hot so beware! Serve the stew from a casserole dish separately. Spoon the couscous onto a plate and ladle the stew on top.

SALADS
&
VEGETABLE DISHES

Here is a delightful range of colourful salads and scrumptious
vegetable dishes and accompaniments. Varied but easy to obtain
ingredients ensure the perfect recipe for every style of meal.

Useful Dressings

A good dressing can make even the simplest combination of fresh vegetables a memorable treat. Remember, in addition to normal salads, lightly cooked hot vegetables such as carrots and potatoes or pulses and grains absorb more flavour and are less greasy if dressed while hot.

Homemade Mayonnaise

Make this by hand, if possible. If you make it in a food processor, it will be noticeably lighter.

2 egg yolks
2.5 ml/½ tsp salt
2.5 ml/½ tsp dry mustard
ground black pepper
300 ml/½ pint/1¼ cups sunflower oil or
  half olive and half sunflower oil
15 ml/1 tbsp wine vinegar
15 ml/1 tbsp hot water

1 Put the yolks into a bowl with the salt and mustard and a grinding of pepper.

2 Stand the bowl on a damp dish cloth. Using a whisk, beat the yolks and the seasoning thoroughly, then beat in a small trickle of oil.

3 Continue trickling in the oil, adding it in very small amounts. The secret of a good, thick mayonnaise is to add the oil very slowly, beating each addition well before you add more. When all the oil is added, mix in the vinegar and hot water.

To make mayonnaise in a blender, use one whole egg and one yolk instead of two yolks. Blend the eggs with the seasonings. Then, with the blades running, trickle in the oil very slowly. Add the vinegar.

Original Thousand Islands Dressing

60 ml/4 tbsp sunflower oil
15 ml/1 tbsp fresh orange juice
15 ml/1 tbsp fresh lemon juice
10 ml/2 tsp grated lemon rind
15 ml/1 tbsp finely chopped onion
5 ml/1 tsp paprika
5 ml/1 tsp Worcestershire sauce
15 ml/1 tbsp finely chopped parsley
salt and ground black pepper

Put all the ingredients into a screw-topped jar, season to taste and shake vigorously. Great with green salads, grated carrot, hot potato, pasta and rice salads.

Yogurt Dressing

150 g/5 oz/⅔ cup natural yogurt
30 ml/2 tbsp mayonnaise
30 ml/2 tbsp milk
15 ml/1 tbsp fresh parsley, chopped
15 ml/1 tbsp fresh chives or spring onions,
  chopped
salt and ground black pepper

Simply mix all the ingredients together thoroughly in a bowl.

Peperonata with Raisins

Sliced roasted peppers in dressing with vinegar-soaked raisins make a tasty side salad which complements many other dishes and is quick to make, especially if you already have a batch of peppers in oil.

SERVES 2–4
90 ml/6 tbsp sliced peppers in olive oil, drained
15 ml/1 tbsp onion, chopped
30 ml/2 tbsp balsamic vinegar
45 ml/3 tbsp raisins
30 ml/2 tbsp fresh parsley, chopped
ground black pepper

1 Toss the peppers with the onion and leave to steep for an hour.

2 Put the vinegar and raisins in a small saucepan and heat for a minute, then allow to cool.

3 Mix all the ingredients together thoroughly and spoon into a serving bowl. Serve lightly chilled.

COOK'S TIP

Peperonata is one of the classic Italian antipasto dishes, served at the start of each meal with crusty bread to mop up the delicious juices. Try serving shavings of fresh Parmesan cheese alongside, or buy a good selection of green and black olives to accompany the peperonata. Small baby tomatoes will complete the antipasto.

Mighty Mushrooms

There is now a wide variety of cultivated mushrooms on sale in larger supermarkets and greengrocers so a simple side dish of mushrooms becomes quite exciting. This also makes an excellent sauce to serve tossed into pasta. Dried ceps or porcini mushrooms are on sale in delicatessens if you have trouble finding them in supermarkets.

SERVES 4

15 g/½ oz pack dried porcini mushrooms/ ceps (optional)
60 ml/4 tbsp olive oil
225 g/8 oz button mushrooms, halved or sliced
115 g/4 oz oyster mushrooms
115 g/4 oz fresh shiitake mushrooms, or 25 g/1 oz dried and soaked mushrooms
2 garlic cloves, crushed
10 ml/2 tsp ground coriander
salt and ground black pepper
45 ml/3 tbsp fresh parsley, chopped

---

1 If you are using porcini mushrooms (and they do give a good rich flavour), soak them in a little hot water just to cover for 20 minutes.

2 In a large saucepan, heat the oil and add all the mushrooms, including the soaked porcinis, if using. Stir well, cover and cook gently for 5 minutes.

3 Stir in the garlic, coriander and seasoning. Cook for another 5 minutes until the mushrooms are tender and much of the liquor has been reduced.

4 Mix in the parsley, allow to cool slightly and serve.

Tomato Sauce

A basic sauce which can either be part of a larger recipe or served as a side sauce. For extra flavour, add red pepper, or ring the changes with orange rind and juice, chopped fresh herbs such as basil, or spice it up with chilli sauce.

SERVES 4–6

1 onion, chopped
2 garlic cloves, crushed
1 small red pepper (optional), chopped
45 ml/3 tbsp olive oil
675 g/1½ lb fresh tomatoes, skinned and chopped or 1 × 400 g/14 oz can chopped tomatoes
15 g/½ oz granulated sugar
salt and ground black pepper
30 ml/2 tbsp fresh herbs, chopped, e.g. basil, parsley, marjoram (optional)

---

1 Gently fry the onion, garlic and red pepper, if using, in the oil for 5 minutes until they are soft.

2 Stir in the tomatoes, add the sugar and seasoning to taste, bring to a boil then cover and simmer for 15–20 minutes.

3 The sauce should now be thick and pulpy. If it is a little thin, then boil it – uncovered – so that it reduces down. Stir in the fresh herbs, if using, and then check the seasoning.

COOK'S TIP

Why not make up a large batch of this sauce and freeze it in two-portion sizes?

Stir-fry Cabbage

An often under-rated vegetable, crisp cabbage is wonderful when lightly cooked the Chinese way in a wok. Any cabbage will do, but perhaps the Savoy cabbage is the nicest.

SERVES 4
½ small cabbage
30 ml/2 tbsp sunflower oil
15 ml/1 tbsp light soy sauce
15 ml/1 tbsp fresh lemon juice (optional)
10 ml/2 tsp caraway seeds
ground black pepper

1 Cut the central core from the cabbage, and shred the leaves finely.

2 Heat the oil until quite hot in a wok and then stir-fry the cabbage for about 2 minutes.

3 Toss in the soy sauce, lemon juice, if using, caraway seeds and pepper, to taste.

Perfect Creamed Potatoes

If a bowl of plain, mashed potatoes sounds boring, then try serving it this way – in the French style. It is absolutely scrumptious!

SERVES 4
1 kg/2 lb potatoes, peeled and diced
45 ml/3 tbsp extra virgin olive oil
about 150 ml/¼ pint/⅔ cup milk
fresh nutmeg, grated
salt and ground black pepper
a few leaves fresh basil or sprigs fresh
  parsley, chopped

COOK'S TIP

Choosing the right potato makes all the difference to creamed or mashed potatoes. A waxy variety won't be light and fluffy, and a potato which breaks down too quickly on boiling will become a slurry when mashed. Most bags of potatoes carry guidelines on what method of cooking they are suited for. In general, red potatoes make a good mash, as do Maris Piper and King Edwards.

1 Boil the potatoes until just tender and not too mushy. Drain very well. Ideally press the potatoes through a special potato 'ricer' (rather like a large garlic press) or mash them well with a potato masher. Do not pass them through a food processor or you will have a gluey mess.

2 Beat the olive oil into the potato and just enough hot milk to make a smooth, thick purée.

3 Flavour to taste with the nutmeg and seasoning then stir in the fresh chopped herbs. Spoon into a warm serving dish and serve as soon as possible.

Oven Chip Roasties

Very popular with children and a much better alternative for all the family to high fat roast potatoes.

SERVES 4–6
4 medium to large baking potatoes
150 ml/¼ pint/⅔ cup olive oil
5 ml/1 tsp dried mixed herbs (optional)
sea salt flakes

1 Preheat the oven to the highest possible temperature, generally 230°C/450°F/Gas 8. Place a lightly-oiled roasting tin in the oven to get really hot.

2 Cut the potatoes in half lengthways then into long thin wedges. Brush each side lightly with oil.

3 When the oven is really hot, remove the pan carefully and scatter the potato slices over it in a single layer.

4 Sprinkle the potatoes with the herbs and salt and place in the oven for about 20 minutes or until they are golden brown, crisp and lightly puffy. Serve immediately.

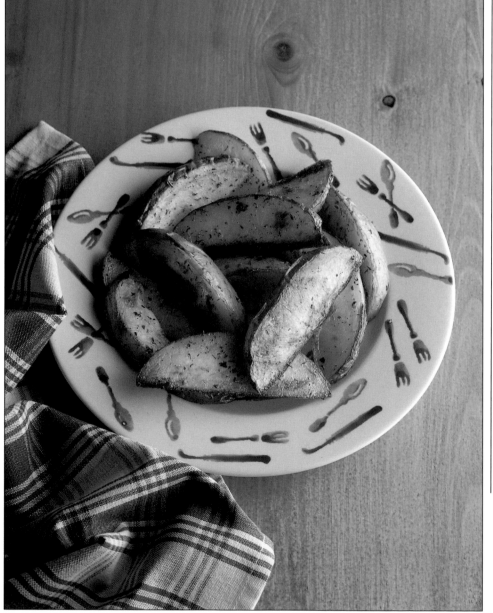

VARIATION

Parsnips also make fine oven chips. Choose large parsnips which tend to have more flavour. Slice thinly on a diagonal and roast in the same way as above, although you may find they do not take as long to cook. They make great mid-week suppers for kids and grown-ups served with fried eggs, mushrooms and tomatoes.

Warm Spicy Dhal

If you thought split yellow peas were only for soups, then try this Indian inspired dish. Serve with rice, chappatis or naan bread and whatever main dish you like. Try eggs, fried aubergines, or even a tasty dish of fried mushrooms.

SERVES 4–6
225 g/8 oz yellow split peas
2 onions, chopped
1 large bay leaf
600 ml/1 pint/2½ cups stock or water
salt and ground black pepper
10 ml/2 tsp black mustard seeds
30 ml/2 tbsp melted butter
1 garlic clove, crushed
2.5 cm/1 in cube fresh root ginger, grated
1 small green pepper, sliced
5 ml/1 tsp ground turmeric
5 ml/1 tsp garam masala or mild curry
  powder
3 tomatoes, skinned and chopped
fresh coriander or parsley, to serve

1 Put the split peas, 1 onion and the bay leaf in the stock or water, in a covered pan. Simmer for 25 minutes, seasoning lightly towards the end.

2 In a separate pan, fry the mustard seeds in the butter for about 30 seconds until they start to pop, then add all the remaining onion, along with the garlic, ginger and green pepper.

3 Sauté for about 5 minutes until softened then stir in the remaining spices and fry for a few seconds more.

4 Add the split peas, tomatoes, and a little extra water if it needs it. Cover and simmer for a further 10 minutes, then check the seasoning and serve hot garnished with coriander or parsley.

Peas and Lettuce

Do not discard the tough, outer leaves of lettuce – they are delicious if shredded and cooked with peas.

SERVES 4
6 outer leaves of lettuce, e.g. Cos, Webbs
1 small onion or shallot, sliced
25 g/1 oz/2 tbsp butter or sunflower margarine
225 g/8 oz frozen garden peas
fresh nutmeg, grated
salt and ground black pepper

1 Pull off the outer lettuce leaves and wash them well. Roughly shred the leaves with your hands.

2 In a saucepan, lightly fry the lettuce and onion or shallot in the butter or margarine for 3 minutes.

3 Add the peas, nutmeg to taste and seasoning. Stir, cover and simmer for about 5 minutes. This dish can be drained or served slightly wet.

Hash Browns

A traditional American breakfast dish, hash browns can be served any time of day. They are a tasty way of using up any left over boiled potatoes.

SERVES 4
60 ml/4 tbsp sunflower or olive oil
about 450 g/1 lb diced, cooked potatoes
1 small onion, chopped
salt and ground black pepper

1 Heat the oil in a large, heavy-based frying pan and when quite hot add the potatoes in a single layer. Scatter the onion on top and season well.

2 Cook on a moderate heat until browned underneath, pressing down on the potatoes with a spoon or spatula to squash them together.

3 When the potatoes are nicely browned, turn them over in sections with a fish slice and fry on the other side, pressing them down once again. Serve when heated through and lightly crispy.

Brussels Sprouts Stir-fry

Brussels sprouts are delicious when quickly stir-fried – they are really full-flavoured and their texture is full of crisp bite. Small Brussels sprouts have the best flavour.

SERVES 6
30 ml/2 tbsp groundnut or sunflower oil
450 g/1 lb small Brussels sprouts, trimmed and halved
3 spring onions, sliced
2 garlic cloves, crushed
1 small yellow pepper, sliced
30 ml/2 tbsp light soy sauce
15 ml/1 tbsp sesame seed oil
good pinch of granulated sugar
ground black pepper
30 ml/2 tbsp sesame seeds, toasted

1 Heat the oil in a wok until quite hot, then stir-fry the sprouts for 2 minutes.

2 Add the spring onions, garlic and yellow pepper and fry for another 2 minutes, stirring.

3 Toss in the soy sauce, sesame seed oil, sugar, and season with pepper. Scatter over the sesame seeds and serve hot immediately.

Hassleback Potatoes

These rather splendid roast potatoes are ideal to serve for dinner partios or special occasions such as Christmas. Use a good quality baking potato for the best results.

SERVES 4
olive or sunflower oil, for roasting
4 medium potatoes, peeled and halved
  lengthways
salt and ground black pepper
15 ml/1 tbsp natural colour dried
  breadcrumbs

1 Pour enough oil into a small roasting pan to just cover the base then put into an oven set at 200°C/400°F/Gas 6 to heat.

2 Meanwhile, par boil the potato halves for 5 minutes then drain. Cool slightly and slash about four times from the rounded tops almost down to the flat bottoms.

3 Place the potatoes in the heated roasting pan and spoon over the hot oil. Season well and return the potatoes to the oven for about 20 minutes.

4 Remove the potatoes once more from the oven, prise open the slashes slightly and spoon over the hot oil. Sprinkle the potato tops lightly with breadcrumbs and return to the oven for another 15 minutes or so until they are golden brown, cooked and crispy.

COOK'S TIP

There are many different ways of roasting potatoes in the oven. First, the choice of potato is important. Choose a variety which holds its shape well and yet is still slightly floury inside. Details on the pack or bag should give you guidance. The oil is important too – choose one which is either flavourless such as sunflower or groundnut oil or one with a lot of good flavour, such as olive oil. Just before serving, try trickling a little sesame seed, walnut or hazelnut oil over the roasted potatoes for a delicious nutty flavour.

PARTIES
&
PICNICS

From informal meals, ideal for outdoor entertaining, to elegant and
delicious dishes that will add style to special occasions, here are
recipes to suit every festivity.

Chargrilled Vegetables with Salsa 🌿

Enjoy a barbecue with these chunky chargrilled vegetables. Serve hot with a no-cook salsa.

SERVES 4
1 large sweet potato, cut in thick slices
2 courgettes, halved lengthways
salt
2 red peppers, quartered
olive oil, to brush
SALSA
2 large tomatoes, skinned and finely chopped
2 spring onions, finely chopped
1 small green chilli, chopped
juice of 1 small lime
30 ml/2 tbsp fresh coriander, chopped
salt and ground black pepper

1 Par-boil the sweet potato for 5 minutes until it is barely tender. Drain and leave to cool.

2 Sprinkle the courgettes with a little salt and leave to drain in a colander for 20 minutes, then pat dry.

3 Make the salsa by mixing all the ingredients together, and allow them to stand for about 30 minutes to mellow.

4 Prepare the barbecue until the coals glow or preheat a grill. Brush the potato slices, courgettes and peppers with oil and cook them until they are lightly charred and softened, brushing with oil again and turning at least once. Serve hot accompanied by the salsa.

Garden Vegetable Terrine

Perfect for a special family picnic or buffet, this is a softly set, creamy terrine of colourful vegetables wrapped in glossy spinach leaves. Select large spinach leaves for the best results.

SERVES 6
225 g/8 oz fresh leaf spinach
3 carrots, cut in sticks
3–4 long, thin leeks
about 115 g/4 oz long green beans, topped and tailed
1 red pepper, cut in strips
2 courgettes, cut in sticks
115 g/4 oz broccoli florets
SAUCE
1 egg and 2 yolks
300 ml/½ pint/1¼ cups single cream
fresh nutmeg, grated
5 ml/1 tsp salt
50 g/2 oz Cheddar cheese, grated
oil, for greasing
ground black pepper

1 Blanch the spinach quickly in boiling water, then drain, refresh in cold water and drain again. Take care not to break up the leaves, then carefully pat them dry.

2 Grease a 1 kg/2 lb loaf tin and line the base with a sheet of greaseproof paper. Line the tin with the spinach leaves, trimming any thick stalks. Allow the leaves to overhang the tin.

3 Blanch the rest of the vegetables in boiling, salted water until just tender. Drain and refresh in cold water then, when cool, pat dry with pieces of kitchen paper towel.

4 Place the vegetables into the loaf tin in a colourful mixture, making sure the sticks of vegetables lie lengthways.

5 Beat the sauce ingredients together and slowly pour over the vegetables. Tap the loaf tin to ensure the sauce seeps into the gaps. Fold over the spinach leaves at the top of the terrine.

6 Cover the terrine with a sheet of greased foil then bake in a roasting pan half full of boiling water at 180°C/350°F/ Gas 4 for about 1–1¼ hours until set.

7 Cool the terrine in the tin then chill. To serve, loosen the sides and shake gently out. Serve cut in thick slices.

Tofu Satay

Grill cubes of tofu until crispy then serve with a Thai-style peanut sauce. Soaking the sticks helps them withstand the hot grilling.

SERVES 4–6
2 × 200 g/7 oz packs smoked tofu
45 ml/3 tbsp light soy sauce
10 ml/2 tsp sesame oil
1 garlic clove, crushed
1 yellow and 1 red pepper, cut in squares
8–12 fresh bay leaves
sunflower oil, for grilling
SAUCE
2 spring onions, finely chopped
2 garlic cloves, crushed
good pinch chilli powder or few drops hot
   chilli sauce
5 ml/1 tsp granulated sugar
15 ml/1 tbsp white vinegar
30 ml/2 tbsp light soy sauce
45 ml/3 tbsp crunchy peanut butter

1 Soak 8–12 wooden satay sticks in water for 20 minutes then drain. Cut the tofu into bite-sized cubes and mix with the soy sauce, sesame oil and garlic. Cover and marinate for 20 minutes.

2 Beat the sauce ingredients together until well blended. Avoid using a food processor for this as the texture should be slightly chunky.

3 Drain the tofu and thread the cubes onto the soaked sticks with the pepper squares and bay leaves. Larger leaves may need to be halved.

4 Heat a grill or barbecue until quite hot. Brush the satays with oil. Grill, turning the sticks occasionally, until the ingredients are browned and crisp. Serve hot with the dipping sauce.

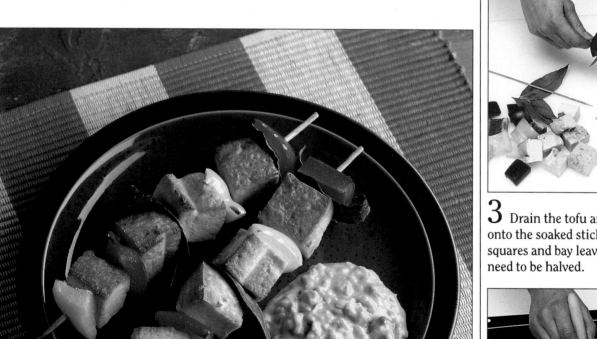

Party Mousaka

Always a popular favourite for both guests and the cook at parties, mousaka is ideal because it benefits from being made ahead of time, requiring just reheating on the day.

SERVES 8
2 large aubergines, thinly sliced
6 courgettes, cut in chunks
150 ml/¼ pint/⅔ cup olive oil, plus extra
  if required
675 g/1½ lb potatoes, thinly sliced
2 onions, sliced
3 garlic cloves, crushed
150 ml/¼ pint/⅔ cup dry white wine
2 × 400 g/14 oz cans chopped tomatoes
30 ml/2 tbsp tomato purée
1 × 430 g/15 oz can green lentils
10 ml/2 tsp dried oregano
60 ml/4 tbsp fresh parsley, chopped
225 g/8 oz/2 cups feta cheese, crumbled
salt and ground black pepper
BECHAMEL SAUCE
40 g/1½ oz/3 tbsp butter
40 g/1½ oz/4 tbsp plain flour
600 ml/1 pint/2½ cups milk
2 eggs, beaten
115 g/4 oz Parmesan cheese, grated
nutmeg, freshly grated

1 Lightly salt the aubergines and courgettes in a colander and leave them to drain for 30 minutes. Rinse and pat dry.

2 Heat the oil until quite hot in a frying pan and quickly brown the aubergine and courgette slices. Remove them with a slotted spoon and drain on a kitchen paper towel. This step is important to cut down on the oiliness of the aubergine. Next, brown the potato slices, remove and pat dry. Add the onion and garlic to the pan with a little extra oil, if required, and fry until lightly browned – 3–5 minutes.

3 Pour in the wine and cook until reduced down then add the tomatoes and lentils plus the liquor from the can. Stir in the herbs and season well. Cover and simmer for 15 minutes.

4 In a large ovenproof dish, layer the vegetables, trickling the tomato and lentil sauce in between and scattering over the feta cheese. Finish with a layer of aubergine slices.

5 Cover the vegetables with a sheet of foil and bake at 190°C/375°F/Gas 5 for 25 minutes or until the vegetables are quite soft but not overcooked.

6 Meanwhile, for the bechamel sauce, put the butter, flour and milk into a saucepan all together and bring slowly to a boil, stirring or whisking constantly. It should thicken and become smooth. Season and add the nutmeg.

7 Remove the sauce and cool for 5 minutes then beat in the eggs. Pour over the aubergines and sprinkle with the Parmesan. If cooking ahead, cool and chill at this stage.

8 To finish, return to the oven uncovered and bake for a further 25–30 minutes until golden and bubbling hot.

Persian Rice and Lentils with a Tahdeeg

Persian or Iran cuisine is an exotic and delicious one, steeped in history. Flavours are intense and exotic, and somehow more sophisticated than other Mediterranean styles. A tahdeeg is the glorious, golden rice crust that forms at the bottom of the saucepan.

SERVES 8
450 g/1 lb basmati rice, rinsed thoroughly and soaked
2 onions, 1 chopped, 1 thinly sliced
2 garlic cloves, crushed
150 ml/¼ pint/⅔ cup sunflower oil
150 g/5 oz/1 cup green lentils, soaked
600 ml/1 pint/2½ cups stock
50 g/2 oz/⅓ cup raisins
10 ml/2 tsp ground coriander
45 ml/3 tbsp tomato purée
salt and ground black pepper
few strands of saffron
1 egg yolk, beaten
10 ml/2 tsp natural yogurt
75 g/3 oz/6 tbsp butter, melted and strained
extra oil, for frying

1 Boil the rinsed and drained rice in plenty of well salted water for 3 minutes only. Drain again.

2 Meanwhile, fry the chopped onion and garlic in 30 ml/2 tbsp of oil for 5 minutes then add the lentils, stock, raisins, coriander, tomato purée and seasoning. Bring to a boil, then cover and simmer for 20 minutes. Set aside.

3 Soak the saffron strands in a little hot water. Remove about 120 ml/8 tbsp of the rice and mix with the egg yolk and yogurt. Season well.

4 In a large saucepan, heat about two-thirds of the remaining oil and scatter the egg and yogurt rice evenly over the base.

5 Scatter the remaining rice into the pan, alternating it with the lentils. Build up in a pyramid shape away from the sides of the pan, finishing with plain rice on top.

6 With a long wooden spoon handle, make three holes down to the bottom of the pan and drizzle over the butter. Bring to a high heat, then wrap the pan lid in a clean, wet tea towel and place firmly on top. When a good head of steam appears, turn the heat down to low. Cook for about 30 minutes.

7 Meanwhile, fry the sliced onion in the remaining oil until browned and crisp. Drain well and set aside.

8 Remove the rice pan from the heat, still covered and stand it briefly in a sink of cold water for a minute or two to loosen the base. Remove the lid and mix a few spoons of the white rice with the saffron water prepared in Step 3.

9 Toss the rice and lentils together in the pan and spoon out onto a serving dish in a mound. Scatter the saffron rice on top. Break up the rice crust on the bottom (the prized tahdeeg) and place around the mound. Scatter the onions on top of the saffron rice and serve.

Birds' Nests

A recipe from an old hand-written cookery book dated 1887. These are also known as Welsh Eggs because they resemble Scotch Eggs but they have leeks in the filling. They are ideal for taking on picnics.

SERVES 6
6 eggs, hard-boiled
flour, seasoned with salt and paprika
1 leek, chopped
10 ml/2 tsp sunflower oil
115 g/4 oz/2 cups fresh white
   breadcrumbs
grated rind and juice of 1 lmeon
50 g/2 oz/½ cup vegetarian shredded suet
60 ml/4 tbsp fresh parsley, chopped
5 ml/1 tsp dried thyme
salt and ground black pepper
1 egg, beaten
75 g/3 oz/½ cup dried breadcrumbs
oil, for deep fat frying
lettuce and tomato slices, to garnish

1 Peel the hard-boiled eggs and toss in the seasoned flour.

2 Fry the leeks in the oil for about 3 minutes. Remove, cool, then mix with the fresh breadcrumbs, lemon rind and juice, suet, herbs and seasoning. If the mixture is a little dry add a little water.

3 Shape the mixture around the eggs, then toss first into the beaten egg, then the dried breadcrumbs. Set aside on a plate to chill for 30 minutes.

4 Pour enough oil to fill one-third of a deep fat fryer and heat to a temperature of 190°C/375°F, and fry the eggs, three at a time, for about 3 minutes. Remove and drain on kitchen paper towel.

5 Serve, cool, cut in half on a platter lined with lettuce and garnished with tomato slices.

Portable Salads

A clever Victorian notion for transporting saucy salads neatly to a picnic site was to pack them in a hollowed out loaf of bread.

SERVES 6
1 large, deep crusty loaf
softened butter or margarine, for spreading
few leaves of crisp lettuce
4 eggs, hardboiled and chopped
350g/12 oz new potatoes, boiled and sliced
1 green pepper, thinly sliced
2 carrots, coarsely grated
3 spring onions, chopped
115 g/4 oz Gouda cheese, grated
salt and ground black pepper
DRESSING
30 ml/2 tbsp mayonnaise
30 ml/2 tbsp natural yogurt
30 ml/2 tbsp milk
1 garlic clove, crushed (optional)
15 ml/1 tbsp fresh dill, chopped

1 Cut the top from the loaf and scoop out the bread inside. Use this for making fresh breadcrumbs and freeze for later.

2 Spread the inside of the loaf lightly with the softened butter or margarine, then line with the lettuce leaves.

3 Mix the eggs with the vegetables and cheese. Season well. Beat the dressing ingredients together and mix into the egg and vegetables.

4 Spoon the dressed salad into the hollow and lined loaf, replace the lid and wrap in cling film. Chill until ready to transport. To serve, spoon the salad onto plates and cut the crust into chunks.

Pan Bagna

You need three essential elements for this French picnic classic: a really fresh French baguette, ripe juicy tomatoes, full of flavour and good, extra virgin olive oil. It is ideal to pack for a picnic.

SERVES 3—4
1 long French stick, split in half
1 garlic clove, halved
60—90 ml/4—6 tbsp extra virgin olive oil
3—4 ripe tomatoes, thinly sliced
salt and ground black pepper
1 small green pepper, thinly sliced
50 g/2 oz Gruyère cheese, thinly sliced
a few stoned black olives, sliced
6 fresh basil leaves

1 Rub the cut surface of the bread with the garlic and discard the clove. Brush over half of the olive oil on both halves of the bread.

2 Lay the tomato slices on top, season well and top with the pepper. Drizzle over the remaining oil.

3 Top the tomatoes with the cheese slices, olives and basil leaves. Sandwich the loaf together firmly and wrap it in cling film for an hour or more. Serve cut diagonally in thick slices.

Sandwiches, Rolls and Fillings

There is an increasing variety of wonderful breads and rolls now for the picnic packer to choose from – not only variations on white and wholemeal breads, but also flavoured breads such as onion, walnut, tomato swirl and black olive. Make sure the breads are fresh and spread them right up to the edges using good butter or a quality margarine spread. Once filled, wrap in cling film and chill until required. However, many a good sandwich is spoiled if served too cold, so allow it to return to room temperature before eating.

FILLING IDEAS
Unless specified, keep the fillings in separate layers rather than mixing the ingredients together.

☐ De-rinded Brie or Camembert, mixed with chopped walnuts or pecans and served with *frisée* or curly endive lettuce.

☐ Yeast extract, scrambled egg (made without milk) and bean sprout (especially good with alfalfa sprouts). Spread the bread or roll with yeast extract rather than mixing it into the egg.

☐ Fry onions in olive oil until crisp and brown. Cool. Layer with shredded, young raw spinach leaves and grated cheese mixed with a little mayonnaise.

☐ **Real English Cucumber Sandwiches.** Peel strips from a whole cucumber to leave it stripy, then slice thinly on a mandoline or a food processor slicer. Sprinkle lightly with salt and leave to drain for 30 minutes in a colander. Pat dry. Sprinkle lightly with a little vinegar and black pepper. Sandwich in very fresh white or wheatmeal bread and cut off the crusts. Cut into small triangles.

DESSERTS & BAKES

Freshly baked breads, cakes and fruit-filled desserts are all utterly irresistible. Here you can also find traditional treats to make Christmas extra special.

Courgette Crown Bread

Adding grated courgettes and cheese to a loaf mixture will keep it tasting fresher for longer. This is a good loaf to serve with a bowl of special soup.

SERVES 8
450 g/1 lb courgettes, coarsely grated
salt
500 g/1¼ lbs/5 cups plain flour
2 sachets fast-action yeast
60 ml/4 tbsp Parmesan cheese, freshly grated
ground black pepper
30 ml/2 tbsp olive oil
lukewarm water, to mix
milk, to glaze
sesame seeds, to garnish

1 Layer the courgettes in a colander and sprinkle them lightly with salt. Leave to drain for 30 minutes, then pat dry.

2 Mix the flour, yeast and Parmesan together and season with black pepper.

3 Stir in the oil and courgettes and add enough lukewarm water to give you a good firm dough.

4 Knead the dough on a lightly floured surface until it is smooth, then return it to the mixing bowl, cover it with oiled cling film and leave it to rise in a warm place.

5 Meanwhile, grease and line a 23 cm/9 in round sandwich tin. Preheat the oven to 200°C/400°F/Gas 6.

6 When the dough has doubled in size, turn it out of the bowl, punch it down and knead it lightly. Break into eight balls, rolling each one and placing them in the tin as shown. Brush the tops with milk and sprinkle over the sesame seeds.

7 Allow to rise again, then bake for 25 minutes or until golden brown. Cool slightly in the tin, then turn out the bread to cool further.

Rosemary Focaccia

Italian flat bread is becoming increasingly popular and very easy to make using packet bread mix. Add traditional ingredients like olives and sun-dried tomatoes.

SERVES 4
450 g/1 lb pack white bread mix
60 ml/4 tbsp extra virgin olive oil
10 ml/2 tsp dried rosemary, crushed
8 sun-dried tomatoes, snipped
12 black olives, stoned and chopped
200 ml/7 fl oz/¾ cup lukewarm water
sea salt flakes

VARIATION

If you want to make your own bread instead of using a bread mix, then use a sachet of easy-blend yeast for each 675 g/1½ lbs/6 cups of flour. Mix the yeast and flour together then add the remaining ingredients as per the recipe.

1 Mix the bread mix with half the oil, the rosemary, tomatoes, olives and water until it forms a firm dough.

2 Turn out the dough onto a lightly floured surface and knead thoroughly for 5 minutes. Return the dough to the mixing bowl and cover with a piece of oiled cling film.

3 Leave the dough to rise in a warm place until it has doubled in size. Meanwhile, lightly grease two baking sheets and preheat the oven to 220°C/425°F/Gas 7.

4 Turn out the risen dough, punch down and knead again. Divide into two and shape into rounds. Place on the baking sheet, and punch hollows in the dough. Trickle over the remaining olive oil and sprinkle with salt.

5 Bake the focaccia for 12–15 minutes until golden brown and cooked. Slide off onto wire racks to cool. Eat slightly warm.

Brown Soda Bread

This is very easy to make – simply mix and bake. Instead of yeast, bicarbonate of soda and cream of tartar are the raising agents. This is an excellent recipe for those new to bread making.

MAKES ONE 1 KG/2 LB LOAF
450 g/1 lb/4 cups plain flour
450 g/1 lb/3 cups wholemeal flour
10 ml/2 tsp salt
15 ml/1 tbsp bicarbonate of soda
20 ml/4 tsp cream of tartar
10 ml/2 tsp caster sugar
50 g/2 oz/4 tbsp butter
up to 900 ml/1½ pints/3¾ cups buttermilk
   or skimmed milk
extra wholemeal flour, to sprinkle

1 Lightly grease a baking sheet. Preheat the oven to 190°C/375°F/Gas 5.

2 Sift all the dry ingredients into a large bowl, tipping any bran from the flour back into the bowl.

3 Rub the butter into the flour mixture, then add enough buttermilk or milk to make a soft dough. You may not need all of it, so add it cautiously.

4 Knead lightly until smooth then transfer to the baking sheet and shape to a large round about 5 cm/2 in thick.

5 Using the floured handle of a wooden spoon, form a large cross on top of the dough. Sprinkle over a little extra wholemeal flour.

6 Bake for 40–50 minutes until risen and firm. Cool for 5 minutes before transferring to a wire rack to cool further.

Cardamom and Saffron Tea Loaf

An aromatic sweet bread ideal for afternoon tea, or lightly toasted for breakfast. Use the sachets of fast action or easy blend yeasts, they make bread making so simple.

MAKES ONE 1 KG/2 LB LOAF
good pinch saffron strands
750 ml/1¼ pints/3 cups lukewarm milk
25 g/1 oz/2 tbsp butter
1 kg/2 lb/8 cups strong plain flour
2 sachets fast action yeast
30 g/1½ oz caster sugar
6 cardamom pods, split open and seeds extracted
115 g/4 oz/⅔ cup raisins
30 ml/2 tbsp clear honey
1 egg, beaten

1 Crush the saffron into a cup containing a little of the warm milk and leave to infuse for 5 minutes.

2 Rub the butter into the flour then mix in the yeast, sugar and cardamom seeds (these may need rubbing to separate them). Stir in the raisins.

3 Beat the remaining milk with the honey and egg, then mix this into the flour along with the saffron milk and strands, stirring well until a firm dough is formed. You may not need all the milk: it depends on the flour.

4 Turn out the dough and knead it on a lightly floured board for about 5 minutes until smooth.

5 Return the dough to the mixing bowl, cover with oiled cling film and leave in a warm place until doubled in size. This could take between 1–3 hours.

VARIATION

For simplicity, leave out the saffron and cardamom and add 10 ml/2 tsp ground cinnamon.

6 Turn the dough out onto a floured board again, punch it down, knead for 3 minutes then shape it into a fat roll and fit it into a greased loaf tin.

7 Cover with a sheet of lightly oiled cling film and stand in a warm place until the dough begins to rise again. Preheat the oven to 200°C/400°F/Gas 6.

8 Bake the loaf for 25 minutes until golden brown and firm on top. Turn out of the tin and as it cools brush the top with honey. Slice when cold and spread with butter. It is also good lightly toasted.

Dinner Milk Rolls

Making bread especially for your dinner guests is not only a wonderful gesture, it is also quite easy to do. You can vary the shapes of the rolls too.

MAKES 12–16
750 g/1½ lb/4 cups strong plain flour
10 ml/2 tsp salt
25 g/1 oz/2 tbsp butter
1 sachet easy-blend fast action yeast
about 450 ml/¾ pint/scant 2 cups
 lukewarm milk
extra cold milk, to glaze
poppy, sesame and sunflower seeds or sea
 salt flakes, to garnish

1 Sift the flour and salt into a large bowl or food processor. Rub in the butter, then mix in the yeast.

2 Mix to a firm dough with the milk, adding it cautiously if the dough is a little dry in case you don't need it all.

3 Knead for at least 5 minutes by hand, or for 2 minutes in a food processor. Place in a bowl, cover with oiled cling film and leave to rise until doubled in size.

4 Turn out of the bowl, punch down and knead again, then break off into 12–16 pieces and either roll each one into a round or make into fun shapes.

5 Place on an oiled baking sheet, glaze the tops with extra milk and sprinkle over seeds or sea salt flakes of your choice.

6 Leave to start rising again, while you preheat the oven to 230°C/450°F/Gas 8. Bake the rolls for 12 minutes or until golden brown and cooked. Cool on a wire rack. Eat the same day, as homemade bread stales quickly.

Indian Pan-fried Breads

Instead of yeast, this dough uses bicarbonate of soda as a raising agent. Traditional Indian spices add a tasty bite to the bread.

MAKES ABOUT 24
250 g/8 oz/2 cups wholemeal flour
250 g/8 oz/2 cups plain flour
5 ml/1 tsp salt
5 ml/1 tsp sugar
10 ml/2 tsp bicarbonate of soda
10 ml/2 tsp cumin seeds
10 ml/2 tsp black mustard seeds
5 ml/1 tsp fennel seeds
450 g/1 lb natural yogurt
75 g/3 oz/6 tbsp vegetable ghee or
 clarified butter
75 ml/5 tbsp sunflower oil

1 Mix the flours with the salt, sugar, bicarbonate of soda and spices. Mix to a firm dough with the yogurt. Be sure to add the yogurt gradually, as you may not need it all.

2 If the dough is too dry, add cold water slowly until you achieve the correct consistency. Cover and chill for 2 hours.

3 Divide the dough into 24 pieces and roll each piece out to a thin round. Stack the rounds under a clean tea towel as you roll out the rest.

4 Fry the breads in the hot ghee or butter and oil, starting with a quarter and adding more ghee/butter and oil each time you fry. Drain the breads well on kitchen paper towel and store under the tea towel. Serve with curries and raitas.

Rich Chocolate Cake

A simple all-in-one cake sandwiched with a simple but very delicious ganache icing. It makes a particularly good special-occasion cake.

SERVES 6–8
115 g/4 oz/1 cup self-raising flour
25 g/1 oz/3 tbsp cocoa
5 ml/1 tsp baking powder
120 g/5 oz/10 tbsp butter, softened, or
   sunflower margarine
120 g/5 oz/¾ cup caster sugar
3 eggs, beaten
30 ml/2 tbsp water
ICING
150 g/5 oz dark (plain) chocolate
150 ml/¼ pint/⅔ cup double cream
5 ml/1 tsp vanilla essence
30 ml/2 tbsp apricot or raspberry jam

1 Grease and line a deep 20 cm/8 in round cake tin. Preheat the oven to 160°C/ 325°F/Gas 3.

2 Put all the cake ingredients into a large bowl or food processor. Beat very well with a wooden spoon or blend in a food processor until the mixture is smooth and creamy.

3 Spoon into the cake tin and bake for about 40–45 minutes or until risen and springy to the touch. Cool upside down on a wire rack for 15 minutes, then turn out and set aside to cool completely.

4 To make the icing, break the chocolate into a heatproof bowl and pour in the cream and vanilla essence. Melt in a microwave on full power for 2–3 minutes, or over a pan of simmering water.

5 Cool the icing, stirring it occasionally and chill lightly until it thickens. Split the cake in half. Spread the jam on one half and half the icing on top of that.

6 Sandwich the two halves together and spread the rest of the icing on top, swirling it attractively or marking it with the tip of a table knife. Decorate as desired with candies or candles – even edible flowers can add a nice touch.

Passion Cake

So called because this is a cake associated with Passion Sunday. The carrot and banana give the cake a rich, moist texture.

SERVES 6—8
200 g/7 oz/1¾ cups self-raising flour
10 ml/2 tsp baking powder
5 ml/1 tsp cinnamon
2.5 ml/½ tsp fresh nutmeg, grated
120 g/5 oz/10 tbsp butter, softened, or
  sunflower margarine
120 g/5 oz/¾ cup soft brown sugar
grated rind of 1 lemon
2 eggs, beaten
2 carrots, coarsely grated
1 ripe banana, mashed
115 g/4 oz/¾ cup raisins
50 g/2 oz/½ cup walnuts or pecans,
  chopped
30 ml/2 tbsp milk
FROSTING
200 g/7 oz cream cheese, softened
30 g/1½ oz icing sugar
juice of 1 lemon
grated rind of 1 orange
6—8 walnuts, halved
coffee crystal sugar, to sprinkle

1 Line and grease a deep 20 cm/8 in cake tin. Preheat the oven to 180°C/350°F/ Gas 4. Sift the flour, baking powder and spices into a bowl.

2 Using an electric mixer, cream the butter and sugar with the lemon rind until it is light and fluffy, then beat in the eggs. Fold in the flour mixture, then the carrots, banana, raisins, nuts and milk.

3 Spoon the mixture into the prepared tin, level the top and bake for about 1 hour until it is risen and the top is springy to touch. Turn the tin upside down and allow the cake to cool in the tin for 30 minutes. Turn onto a wire rack.

4 When cold, split the cake in half. Cream the cheese with the icing sugar, lemon juice and orange rind, then sandwich the two halves together with half of the frosting.

5 Spread the rest of the frosting on top, swirling it attractively. Decorate with the walnut halves and sprinkle with the coffee crystal sugar.

Yogurt with Apricots and Pistachios

If you allow a thick yogurt to drain overnight, it becomes even thicker and more luscious. Add honeyed apricots and nuts and you have an exotic yet simple dessert.

SERVES 4
450 g/1 lb Greek-style yogurt
175 g/6 oz/⅔ cup no-need-to-soak dried apricots, snipped
15 ml/1 tbsp clear honey
orange rind, grated
30 ml/2 tbsp unsalted pistachios, roughly chopped
ground cinnamon

VARIATION

For a simple dessert, strain the fruit, cover with yogurt and sprinkle with demerara sugar and a little mixed spice or cinnamon.

1 Place the yogurt in a fine sieve and allow it to drain overnight in the fridge over a bowl.

2 Discard the whey from the yogurt. Place the apricots in a saucepan, barely cover with water and simmer for just 3 minutes, to soften. Drain and cool, then mix with the honey.

3 Mix the yogurt with the apricots, orange rind and nuts. Spoon into sundae dishes, sprinkle over a little cinnamon and chill.

Fresh Pineapple Salad 🌿

Very refreshing, this salad can be prepared ahead. Orange flower water is available from Middle Eastern food stores or good delicatessens.

SERVES 4
1 small ripe pineapple
icing sugar, to taste
15 ml/1 tbsp orange flower water, or more if liked
115 g/4 oz/good ½ cup fresh dates, stoned and quartered
225 g/8 oz fresh strawberries, sliced
few fresh mint sprigs, to serve

1 Cut the skin from the pineapple and, using the tip of a vegetable peeler, remove as many brown 'eyes' as possible. Quarter lengthways, remove the core then slice.

2 Lay the pineapple in a shallow, pretty, glass bowl. Sprinkle with sugar and orange flower water.

3 Add the dates and strawberries to the pineapple, cover and chill for a good 2 hours, stirring once or twice. Serve lightly chilled decorated with a few mint sprigs.

Walnut and Raspberry Meringue

Make sure you beat the egg whites stiffly to form a good firm foam for the meringue. When you fold in the nuts the meringue will hold its shape. Assemble this dish just before serving, if at all possible.

SERVES 4–6
3 egg whites
few drops of fresh lemon juice
175 g/6 oz/1 cup caster sugar
75 g/3 oz/¾ cup walnuts, finely chopped
450 g/1 lb fresh raspberries
200 ml/7 fl oz/¾ cup crème frâiche or
   double cream
few drops vanilla essence
icing sugar, to taste

1 Preheat the oven to 160°C/325°F/ Gas 3. Draw three 20 cm/8 in circles on non-stick baking parchment. Place the circles on baking sheets.

COOK'S TIP

Don't waste egg whites if you have recipes which call for yolks only. They do freeze very well and can be stored in batches of 3 or 4 whites at a time. In fact, when thawed, frozen egg whites make a much better foam.

2 Whisk the egg whites in a spotlessly clean and grease-free bowl with the few drops of lemon juice. (This gives a more stable foam).

3 When the whites are softly stiff, gradually whisk in the sugar until thick and glossy. Quickly and carefully fold in the nuts.

4 Spread or pipe the mixture onto the three paper circles. Bake for 40–50 minutes until firm and crisp on top. This may have to be done in batches.

5 Cool on a wire rack and peel off the paper. Store in an airtight container until ready to serve.

6 Whip the crème frâiche or cream with the vanilla and sugar, until the mixture is quite stiff.

7 Reserve a few raspberries for decoration, crush those remaining and mix into the creamy cheese mixture.

8 Spread the fruit cream on the three meringues. Sandwich them together and decorate the top layer with the reserved raspberries.

Rum-Baked Bananas

This is a quick, hot pudding which bakes in just minutes. When cooked, bananas have a really full flavour that is enhanced by rum and orange. Serve this dish with a trickle of cream.

SERVES 4
4 bananas
grated rind and juice of 1 orange
30 ml/2 tbsp dark rum
50 g/2 oz/¼ cup soft brown sugar (optional)
good pinch of ground ginger
fresh nutmeg, grated
40 g/1½ oz/3 tbsp butter

1 Preheat the oven to 180°C/350°F/Gas 4. Peel the bananas and slice them into four large ramekins.

2 Spoon the orange juice and rum over the sliced bananas. Sprinkle over the sugar, if using, orange rind and spices. Dot with butter.

3 Cover the ramekins with small pieces of foil or buttered papers and bake for 15 minutes. Allow to cool slightly before serving with cream or natural yogurt.

Muesli Bars

Instead of buying expensive crunchy oat bars, bake your own. They are much nicer and really quite easy to make. Use muesli with no added sugar for the bars.

MAKES 12–16
350 g/12 oz/4 cups muesli
75 ml/5 tbsp sunflower oil
75 ml/5 tbsp clear honey
5 ml/1 tsp mixed spice
1 egg, beaten
30 g/1½ oz molasses sugar (optional)

COOK'S TIP

To make your own muesli, buy bags of flaked grains and oats from your local health food store. As these will make a large amount, you need to make sure you eat a lot of muesli! Choose jumbo porridge oats, barley flakes and wheat flakes, then add seeds, dried fruits and nuts of your choice.

1 Preheat the oven to 160°C/325°F/Gas 3. Grease and line a shallow baking tin about 18 × 28 cm/7 × 11 in.

2 Mix all the ingredients together and spoon into the tin, patting the mixture until it is level.

3 Bake for 30–35 minutes until light brown round the edges. Remove, cool slightly then mark into 12–16 pieces.

4 Cool completely, turn out onto a wire rack and break into the marked pieces. Store in an airtight tin.

Oatmeal and Date Brownies

These brownies are marvellous for special brunches or as a tea time treat. The secret of chewy, moist brownies is not to overcook them.

MAKES 16
150 g/5 oz dark (plain) chocolate
50 g/2 oz/4 tbsp butter
75 g/3 oz/¾ cup quick-cook porridge oats
25 g/1 oz/3 tbsp wheat germ
25 g/1 oz/⅓ cup milk powder
2.5 ml/½ tsp baking powder
2.5 ml/½ tsp salt
50 g/2 oz/½ cup walnuts, chopped
50 g/2 oz/⅓ cup dates, chopped
50 g/2 oz/¼ cup molasses sugar
5 ml/1 tsp vanilla essence
2 eggs, beaten

1 Break the chocolate into a heatproof bowl and add the butter. Melt it either in a microwave on full power for 2 minutes, stirring once, or in a pan over very gently simmering water.

2 Cool the chocolate, stirring it occasionally. Grease and line a 20 cm/8 in square cake tin. Preheat the oven to 180°C/350°F/Gas 4.

3 Combine all the dry ingredients together in a bowl then beat in the melted chocolate, vanilla and eggs.

4 Pour the mixture into the prepared cake tin, level the top and bake for about 20–25 minutes until it is firm around the edges yet still soft in the centre.

5 Cool the brownies in the tin then chill them. When they are more solid, turn them out of the tin and cut into 16 squares. Store in an airtight tin.

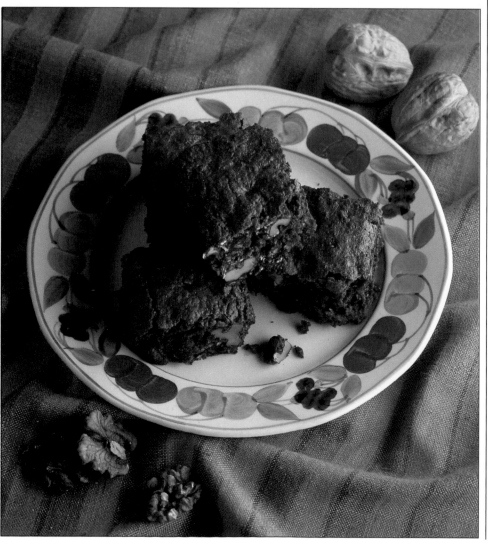

COOK'S TIP

These make a marvellous lunch box or picnic snack, and if you store them for a day or two before eating they will become more moist and even more chewy.

Cut-and-Come-Again Fruit Cake

A rich fruit cake keeps well for quite some time so it is ideal to have one on hand for when you feel like a slice of something sweet or when guests drop in unexpectedly.

SERVES 8–10
225 g/8 oz/1 cup butter, softened, or sunflower margarine
225 g/8 oz/1 cup soft brown sugar
4 eggs, beaten
15 ml/1 tbsp black treacle
350 g/12 oz/3 cups plain flour
5 ml/1 tsp mixed spice
45 ml/3 tbsp milk
900 g/2 lb dried mixed fruit (e.g. raisins, currants, cherries)
50 g/2 oz/½ cup flaked almonds
grated rind of 1 lemon
a few blanched almond halves (optional)
a little milk, to glaze (optional)
30 ml/2 tbsp brandy or rum (optional)

1 Preheat the oven to 140°C/275°F/ Gas 1. Grease and line a deep 20 cm/8 in cake tin with doubled greaseproof paper.

2 Cream the butter or margarine and sugar until light and fluffy. Beat in the eggs with the treacle and stir into the creamed mixture.

3 Sift the flour and spice and fold this into the mixture, alternating it with the milk. Stir in the dried fruit, almonds and lemon rind.

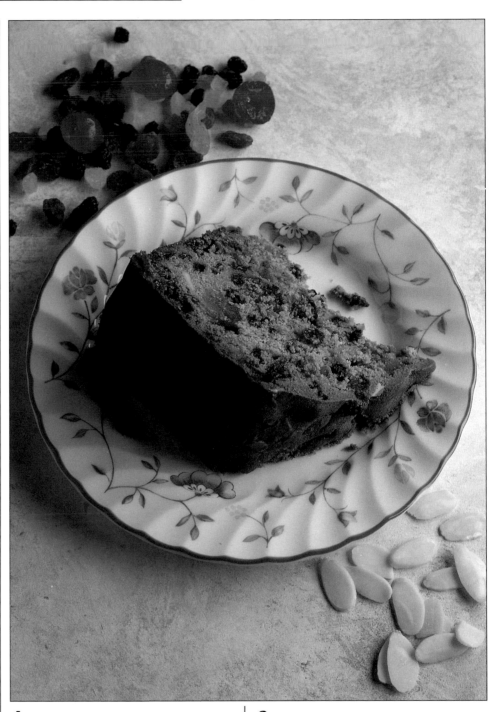

4 Spoon the mixture into the prepared tin. If liked, dip the almond halves in a little milk and arrange them on top.

5 Bake on a shelf one position below the centre of the oven for about 3 hours. When cooked, the top of the cake will feel quite firm and a skewer inserted into the centre will come out clean.

6 Allow the cake to cool for 10 minutes then, if using the brandy or rum, make small holes in the top of the cake with a thin skewer. Slowly pour the spirit over the cake.

7 Allow the cake to cool completely in the tin, then turn it out and remove the paper. Wrap it in clean greaseproof paper and foil or store in an airtight container for one week before cutting.

Thai Rice Cake

A celebration gâteau made from fragrant Thai rice covered with a tangy cream icing. Top with fresh berry fruits or pipe on a greeting in melted chocolate. This is a good cake to serve to those with a gluten allergy as it is flour free.

SERVES 8–10
225 g/8 oz/1¼ cups Thai fragrant or Jasmine rice
1 litre/1¾ pints/4½ cups milk
115 g/4 oz/¾ cup caster sugar
6 cardamom pods, crushed open
2 bay leaves
300 ml/½ pint/1¼ cups whipping cream
6 eggs, separated
TOPPING
300 ml/½ pint/1¼ cups double cream
200 g/7 oz quark
5 ml/1 tsp vanilla essence
grated rind of 1 lemon
30 g/1½ oz caster sugar
soft berry fruits and sliced star or kiwi fruits, to decorate

2 Return the rice to the pan with the milk, sugar, cardamom and bay leaves. Bring to the boil, then lower the heat and simmer the mixture for 20 minutes, stirring it occasionally.

4 Whisk the egg whites until they are softly stiff and fold into the rice mixture. Spoon into the prepared tin and bake for 45–50 minutes until risen and golden brown. The centre should be slightly wobbly – it will firm up as it cools.

5 Chill overnight in the tin. Turn out on to a large serving plate. Whip the double cream until stiff then mix in the quark, vanilla essence, lemon rind and sugar.

1 Grease and line a deep 25 cm/10 in round cake tin. Boil the rice in unsalted water for 3 minutes then drain.

3 Allow the mixture to cool, then remove the bay leaves and any cardamom husks. Turn into a bowl. Beat in the cream and then the egg yolks. Preheat the oven to 180°C/350°F/Gas 4.

VARIATION

If you prefer something simpler, turn the cake out and top with sliced fruits or a lovely tumble of berries and stoned cherries. Serve the topping separately, thinning it down slightly with a little milk.

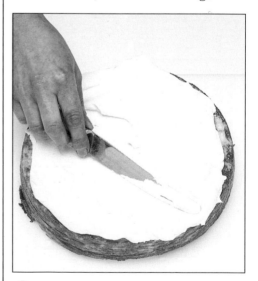

6 Cover the top and sides of the cake with the cream, swirling it attractively. Decorate with soft berry fruits and sliced star or kiwi fruits.

Apple and Apricot Crumble 🌿

Lightly cook the fruit base first for the best results. That way you'll get a delicious contrast between soft fruit and crunchy topping.

SERVES 4—6
1 × 425 g/15 oz can apricot halves in natural juice
450 g/1 lb cooking apples, peeled and sliced
granulated sugar, to taste (optional)
grated rind of 1 orange
fresh nutmeg, grated
TOPPING
200 g/7 oz/1¾ cups plain flour
50 g/2 oz/½ cup rolled porridge oats
120 g/5 oz/10 tbsp butter or sunflower margarine
50 g/2 oz/¼ cup soft brown sugar
demerara sugar, to sprinkle

1 Preheat the oven to 190°C/375°F/ Gas 5. Drain the apricots, reserving a little of the juice.

2 Put the apples into a saucepan with a little of the reserved apricot juice and sugar to taste. Simmer for just 5 minutes to cook the fruit lightly.

3 Transfer the apples into an ovenproof pie dish and stir in the apricots, orange rind and nutmeg to taste.

4 Rub the flour, oats and butter or margarine together until they form fine crumbs. (You can use a food processor if you prefer.) Mix in the soft brown sugar.

5 Scatter the crumble over the fruit, spreading it evenly. Sprinkle with a little demerara sugar. Bake for about 30 minutes until golden and crisp on top. Allow to cool slightly before serving.

French Apple Cake

With its moist texture and fruity flavour, this cake is ideal to serve as a dessert accompanied by a little cream or fromage frais.

SERVES 6–8
450 g/1 lb cooking apples or tart dessert
   apples, cored and chopped
115 g/4 oz/1 cup self-raising flour
5 ml/1 tsp baking powder
115 g/4 oz/⅔ cup caster sugar
90 ml/6 tbsp milk
50 g/2 oz/4 tbsp butter, melted
3 eggs
5 ml/1 tsp fresh nutmeg, grated
TOPPING
75 g/3 oz/6 tbsp butter, softened, or
   sunflower margarine
115 g/4 oz/½ cup caster sugar
5 ml/1 tsp vanilla essence
sifted icing sugar, to dust

1 Preheat the oven to 160°C/325°F/ Gas 3. Grease and line the base of a deep 23 cm/9 in round cake tin.

2 Put the chopped apples into the base of the cake tin.

3 Put all the remaining cake ingredients, except 1 egg, into a bowl or food processor. Beat to a smooth batter.

4 Pour the batter over the apples in the tin, level the top then bake for 40–45 minutes until lightly golden.

5 Meanwhile, cream the topping ingredients together with the remaining egg. Remove the cake from the oven and spoon over the topping.

6 Return the cake to the oven for a further 20–25 minutes until it is golden brown. Cool the cake in the tin, then turn it out and finish with a light dusting of icing sugar.

VARIATION

We don't use fresh fruit very often in cake mixtures, which is a pity as it gives a delightful flavour. Try adding finely chopped pears or pineapple, or even raspberries.

Halva

The Greeks love homemade halva which they cook in a saucepan with semolina, olive oil, sugar, honey and almonds. You can either eat it warm, or allow it to set and cut it into slices or squares.

MAKES 12–16 PIECES
400 g/14 oz/2 cups granulated sugar
1 litre/1¾ pints/4½ cups water
2 cinnamon sticks
225 ml/8 fl oz/1 cup olive oil
350 g/12 oz/3 cups semolina
75 g/3 oz/¾ cup blanched almonds, 6–8 halved, the rest chopped
120 ml/4 fl oz/½ cup clear honey
ground cinnamon, to serve

1 Reserve 60 ml/4 tbsp sugar and dissolve the rest in the water over a gentle heat, stirring from time to time.

2 Add the cinnamon sticks, bring to a boil then simmer for 5 minutes. Cool and remove the cinnamon sticks.

3 Heat the olive oil in a large heavy-based saucepan and, when it is quite hot, stir in the semolina. Cook, stirring occasionally, until it turns a golden brown, then add the chopped almonds and cook for a further minute or so.

4 Keep the heat low and stir in the syrup, taking care as the semolina may spit. Bring the mixture to a boil, stirring it constantly. When it is just smooth, remove the pan from the heat and stir in the honey.

5 Cool slightly and mix in the reserved sugar. Pour the halva into a greased and lined shallow tin, pat it down and mark into squares.

6 Sprinkle the halva lightly with ground cinnamon and fix one almond half on each square. When set, cut up and serve.

Rice Condé Sundae

Cook a rice pudding on top of the stove instead of in the oven for a light creamy texture which is particularly good served cold topped with fruits, toasted nuts and even a trickle of hot chocolate sauce.

SERVES 4
50 g/2 oz/⅓ cup pudding rice
600 ml/1 pint/2½ cups milk
5ml/1 tsp vanilla essence
2.5 ml/½ tsp ground cinnamon
30 g/1½ oz granulated sugar
TO SERVE
Choose from: strawberries, raspberries or
   blueberries
chocolate sauce
flaked toasted almonds

1 Put the rice, milk, vanilla essence, cinnamon and sugar into a medium-sized saucepan. Bring to the boil, stirring constantly, and then turn down the heat to a gentle simmer.

2 Cook the rice for about 30–40 minutes, stirring occasionally. Add extra milk if it reduces down too quickly.

3 Make sure the grains are soft, then remove the pan from the heat and allow the rice to cool, stirring it occasionally. When cold, chill the rice in the refrigerator.

4 Just before serving, stir the rice and spoon into four sundae dishes. Top with fruits, chocolate sauce and almonds.

VARIATION

Milk puddings are at last enjoying something of a comeback in popularity. Instead of simple pudding rice try using a Thai fragrant or Jasmine rice for a delicious natural flavour. For a firmer texture, an Italian Arborio rice makes a good pudding too.

There's no need to use a lot of high-fat milk or cream either. A pudding made with semi-skimmed or even fat-free milk can be just as nice and is much more healthy.

Three-fruits Compôte 🍃

Mixing dried fruits with fresh ones makes a good combination, especially if flavoured delicately with a little orange flower water. A melon-ball scoop gives the compôte a classy touch, but you could chop the melon into cubes.

SERVES 6
175 g/6 oz/1 cup dried, no-need-to-soak apricots
1 small ripe pineapple
1 small ripe melon
15 ml/1 tbsp orange flower water

1 Put the apricots into a saucepan with 300 ml/½ pint water. Bring to the boil, then simmer for 5 minutes. Leave to cool.

2 Peel and quarter the pineapple then cut the core from each quarter and discard. Cut the flesh into chunks.

3 Seed the melon and scoop balls from the flesh. Save any juices which fall from the fruits and tip them into the apricots.

4 Stir in the orange flower water and mix all the fruits together. Pour into an attractive serving dish and chill lightly before serving.

VARIATION

A good fruit salad needn't be a boring mixture of multi-coloured fruits swimming in sweet syrup. Instead of the usual apple, orange and grape type of salad, give it a theme, such as red berry fruits or a variety of sliced green fruits – even a dish of just one fruit nicely prepared and sprinkled lightly with some sugar and fresh lemon juice can look beautiful and tastes delicious. Do not use more than three fruits in a salad so that the flavours remain distinct.

Red Berry Tart with Lemon Cream Filling

Just right for warm summer days, this flan is best filled just before serving so the pastry remains mouth-wateringly crisp. Select red berry fruits such as strawberries, raspberries or redcurrants.

SERVES 6–8
150 g/5 oz/1¼ cups plain flour
25 g/1 oz/¼ cup cornflour
30 g/1½ oz icing sugar
100 g/3½ oz/8 tbsp butter
5 ml/1 tsp vanilla essence
2 egg yolks, beaten
FILLING
200 g/7 oz cream cheese, softened
45 ml/3 tbsp lemon curd
grated rind and juice of 1 lemon
icing sugar, to sweeten (optional)
225 g/8 oz mixed red berry fruits
45 ml/3 tbsp redcurrant jelly

1 Sift the flour, cornflour and icing sugar together, then rub in the butter until the mixture resembles breadcrumbs. This can be done in a food processor.

2 Beat the vanilla into the egg yolks, then mix into the crumbs to make a firm dough, adding cold water if necessary.

3 Roll out and line a 23 cm/9 in round flan tin, pressing the dough well up the sides after trimming. Prick the base of the flan with a fork and allow it to rest in the refrigerator for 30 minutes.

4 Preheat the oven to 200°C/400°F/ Gas 6. Line the flan with greaseproof paper and baking beans. Place the tin on a baking sheet and bake for 20 minutes, removing the paper and beans for the last 5 minutes. When cooked, cool and remove the pastry case from the flan tin.

VARIATION

There are all sorts of delightful variations to this recipe. For instance, leave out the redcurrant jelly and sprinkle lightly with icing sugar or decorate with fresh mint leaves. Alternatively, top with sliced kiwi fruits or bananas.

5 Cream the cheese, lemon curd and lemon rind and juice, adding icing sugar to sweeten, if you wish. Spread the mixture into the base of the flan.

6 Top the flan with the fruits. Warm the redcurrant jelly and trickle it over the fruits just before serving.

Honey and Lemon Spicy Mincemeat

Like Christmas Pudding, mincemeat is best made a few weeks ahead to allow the flavours to mature. This mixture is lighter than most traditional recipes.

MAKES 1.5 KG/3 LB
150 g/6 oz/1 cup vegetarian shredded suet
225 g/8 oz/1½ cups currants
1 large cooking apple, coarsely grated
grated rind of 2 lemons
grated rind and juice of 1 orange
115 g/4 oz/¾ cup no-need-to-soak prunes, chopped
115 g/4 oz/¾ cup stoned dates, chopped
150 g/6 oz/1 cup raisins
225 g/8 oz/1¼ cups sultanas
115 g/4 oz/1 cup flaked almonds
90 ml/6 tbsp clear honey
60 ml/4 tbsp brandy or rum
5 ml/1 tsp mixed spice
2.5 ml/½ tsp ground cloves or all-spice

1 Mix all the ingredients together well in a large mixing bowl. Cover and store in a cool place for two days, stirring the mixture occasionally.

2 Sterilize clean jam jars by placing them in a warm oven for 30 minutes. Cool, then fill with mincemeat, and seal with wax discs and screw tops. Label and store until required.

Cinnamon and Treacle Cookies

The smell of homemade cookies baking is bettered only by their wonderful taste! These cookies are slightly sticky, spicy and nutty.

MAKES 24
30 ml/2 tbsp black treacle
50 g/2 oz/4 tbsp butter or margarine
115 g/4 oz/1 cup plain flour
1.25 ml/¼ tsp bicarbonate of soda
2.5 ml/½ tsp ground ginger
5 ml/1 tsp ground cinnamon
40 g/1½ oz/¼ cup soft brown sugar
15 ml/1 tbsp ground almonds or hazelnuts
1 egg yolk
115 g/4 oz/1 cup icing sugar, sifted

1 Heat the treacle and butter or margarine until it just begins to melt.

2 Sift the flour into a large bowl with the bicarbonate of soda and spices, then stir in the sugar and almonds or nuts.

3 Beat the treacle mixture briskly into the bowl together with the egg yolk and draw the ingredients together to form a firm but soft dough.

4 Roll the dough out on a lightly floured surface to a 5 mm/¼ in thickness and stamp out shapes, such as stars, hearts or circles. Re-roll the trimmings for more shapes. Place on a very lightly greased baking sheet and chill for 15 minutes.

5 Meanwhile, preheat the oven to 190°C/375°F/Gas 5. Prick the cookies lightly with a fork and bake them for 12–15 minutes until just firm. Cool on wire trays to crisp up.

6 To decorate, mix the icing sugar with a little lukewarm water to make it slightly runny, then drizzle it over the biscuits on the wire tray.

Mince Pies with Orange Cinnamon Pastry

Homemade mince pies are so much nicer than shop bought, especially with a flavoursome pastry.

MAKES 18
225 g/8 oz/2 cups plain flour
30 g/1½ oz icing sugar
10 ml/2 tsp ground cinnamon
120 g/5 oz/10 tbsp butter
grated rind of 1 orange
about 60 ml/4 tbsp ice cold water
225 g/8 oz/1½ cups vegetarian
   mincemeat
1 beaten egg, to glaze
icing sugar, to dust

1 Sift together the flour, icing sugar and cinnamon then rub in the butter until it forms crumbs. (This can be done in a food processor.) Stir in the grated orange rind.

2 Mix to a firm dough with the ice cold water. Knead lightly, then roll out to a 5 mm/¼ in thickness.

3 Using a 7 cm/2½ in round cutter, cut out 18 circles, re-rolling as necessary. Then cut out 18 smaller 5 cm/2 in circles. If liked, cut out little shapes from the centre of the smaller circles.

4 Line two bun tins with the 18 larger circles – they will fill one and a half tins. Spoon a small spoonful of mincemeat into each pastry case and top with the smaller pastry circles, pressing the edges lightly together to seal.

5 Glaze the tops of the pies with egg and leave to rest in the refrigerator for 30 minutes. Preheat the oven to 200°C/400°F/Gas 6.

6 Bake the pies for 15–20 minutes until they are golden brown. Remove them to wire racks to cool. Serve just warm and dusted with icing sugar.

Christmas Pudding

If possible, try to make your puddings at least one month before Christmas for the flavours to develop and mature. Dried prunes and apricots add an unusual texture and delicious flavour to this recipe.

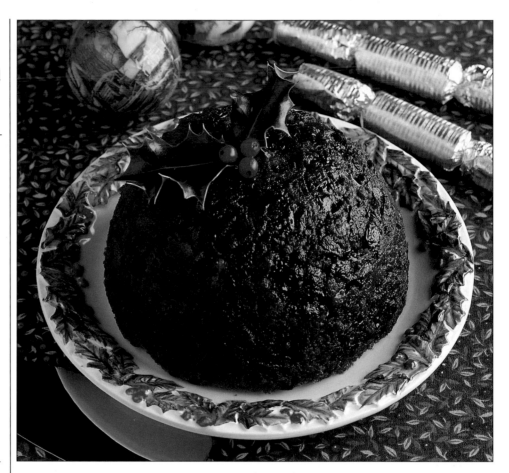

MAKES TWO 1 LITRE/2 PINT PUDDINGS
275 g/10 oz/5 cups fresh white breadcrumbs
225 g/8 oz/2 cups shredded vegetarian suet or ice cold butter, coarsely grated
115 g/4 oz/1 cup plain flour
225 g/8 oz/1 cup soft brown sugar
10 ml/2 tsp ground mixed spice
350 g/12 oz/2½ cups currants
350 g/12 oz/2½ cups raisins
225 g/8 oz/1¾ cups sultanas
150 g/6 oz/1 cup stoned no-need-to-soak prunes, chopped
115 g/4 oz/¾ cup no-need-to-soak dried apricots, chopped
115 g/4 oz/¾ cup candied peel, chopped
115 g/4 oz/¾ cup glacé cherries, washed and chopped
rind of 1 large lemon, grated
4 eggs, beaten
30 ml/2 tbsp black treacle
150 ml/¼ pint/⅔ cup beer or milk
60 ml/4 tbsp brandy or rum

1 Grease two 1 litre/2 pint pudding basins and line the bases with small discs of greaseproof paper.

2 Mix all the ingredients together well. If you intend to put lucky coins or tokens in the mixture, boil them first to ensure they are clean and wrap them in foil.

3 Pack the mixture into the two basins, pushing it down lightly.

4 Cover each pudding with greased greaseproof paper and a double thickness of foil. Secure it round the rim with kitchen string.

5 Place two old china saucers in the base of two large saucepans. Stand the basins on the saucers, pour boiling water to come two thirds of the way up and boil gently for about 6 hours, checking the water level regularly and topping it up with more boiling water.

6 When cooked, cool the puddings, remove the foil and paper then re-cover to store. On Christmas Day, re-boil for about 2 hours and serve with brandy butter and cream or custard.

Index